THE CARTOON GUIDE TO
U.S. HISTORY

Volume II
1865-NOW

Also available by Larry Gonick

The Cartoon Guide to Genetics
(with Mark Wheelis)

The Cartoon Guide to Computer Science

The Cartoon Guide to U.S. History:
Volume I, 1585–1865

THE CARTOON GUIDE TO

U.S. HISTORY

Volume II
1865-NOW

Larry Gonick

BARNES & NOBLE BOOKS
A DIVISION OF HARPER & ROW, PUBLISHERS
New York, Cambridge, Philadelphia
San Francisco, Washington, London, Mexico City
São Paulo, Singapore, Sydney

Portions of this work originally appeared in *Whole Earth Review*.

FIRST EDITION

Library of Congress Cataloging-in-Publication Data
Gonick, Larry.
    The cartoon guide to U.S. history.

    (College outline series)
    "Portions...have appeared in Whole Earth Review"—T.p. verso.
    Bibliography: p.
    Includes index.
    Contents: v. 1. 1585–1865.
                v. 2. 1865–now.
    1. United States—History, Comic, satirical, etc.   I. Title.   II.Title:
Cartoon guide to United States history.   III. Series.
E178.4.G66   1987   973'.0207   85-45200
ISBN 0-06-460420-9 (pbk. : v.1)
ISBN 0-06-460421-7 (pbk. : v. 2)

88 89 90 91 92 MPC 10 9 8 7 6 5 4 3 2 1

CONTENTS

THE CARTOON GUIDE TO
U.S. HISTORY

Volume II
1865-NOW

INTRODUCTION
TO VOLUME II

In BOOKS, MOVIES, AND ON THE IMMORTAL TUBE, THE CIVIL WAR IS PORTRAYED AS A WAR BETWEEN NORTH AND SOUTH — WHICH IT WAS...

...AS A WAR BETWEEN BROTHERS, WHICH IT WAS...

...AS A WAR TO PRESERVE THE UNION, WHICH IT WAS...

But THE CIVIL WAR WAS ALSO SOMETHING ELSE: A WAR BETWEEN TWO SYSTEMS...

(PERHAPS THIS IDEA IS TOO COMPLEX FOR MOST BOOKS, MOVIES, AND MINISERIES.)

LUCKILY, THIS IS A COMIC BOOK, FOR WHICH NO IDEA IS TOO COMPLEX!

ONE SYSTEM — THE LOSER — WAS THE **SLAVE SYSTEM.** IT WAS AN OLD SYSTEM, AS OLD AS ANCIENT EGYPT, AT LEAST, AND DEFINITELY ON ITS LAST LEGS BY THE 1850's.

UNDER THE SLAVE SYSTEM, THE WORKER WAS THE PROPERTY OF THE MASTER, RATHER LIKE AN INTELLIGENT KIND OF LIVESTOCK.

THE MASTERS FORMED A SMALL ELITE WITH IMMENSE POWER — THOUGH RELATIVELY LITTLE MONEY. MOST OF THEIR WEALTH WAS TIED UP IN LAND AND HUMAN BEINGS.

THE WINNING SYSTEM
ADVERTISED ITSELF AS THE
**oo SYSTEM OF
FREE LABOR. oo**
UNDER THIS SYSTEM,
THE CITIZEN-WORKER
WAS SUPPOSED TO BE
FREE TO WORK OR NOT
TO WORK, FREE TO
BARGAIN FOR WAGES,
FREE TO QUIT, FREE
TO HEAD WESTWARD...

FREE TO
BE ME !!

AS PREACHED — AND PRACTICED — BY ABRAHAM LINCOLN,
THIS WAS THE AMERICAN DREAM: BEGIN AS A HIRED
HAND, THEN BY DINT OF HARD WORK, THRIFT, AND
OPPORTUNITY, RISE TO BECOME AN INDEPENDENT BUSINESSMAN,
FARMER, OR (IN LINCOLN'S CASE) LAWYER.

IF YOU DON'T
MAKE IT, IT'S
YER OWN DANG
FAULT!

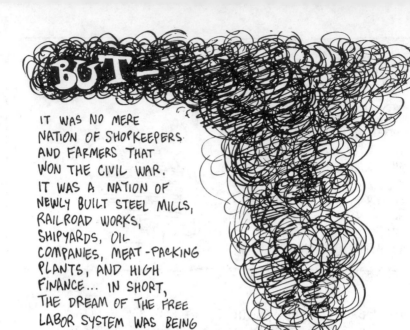

BUT—

IT WAS NO MERE NATION OF SHOPKEEPERS AND FARMERS THAT WON THE CIVIL WAR. IT WAS A NATION OF NEWLY BUILT STEEL MILLS, RAILROAD WORKS, SHIPYARDS, OIL COMPANIES, MEAT-PACKING PLANTS, AND HIGH FINANCE... IN SHORT, THE DREAM OF THE FREE LABOR SYSTEM WAS BEING REALIZED AS MODERN

INDUSTRIAL CAPITALISM.

COUGH!

THE INDUSTRIALISTS AND FINANCIERS AMASSED WEALTH BEYOND A SLAVE OWNER'S WILDEST DREAMS: ONE MAN COULD CONTROL AN ENTIRE INDUSTRY, COULD OWN MINES, FACTORIES, STOCKS, BONDS, MANSIONS, YACHTS, GOLD, SENATORS...

WHY WASTE MONEY BUYING WORKERS?

4

THIS RAISED MANY QUESTIONS FOR THE AMERICAN PEOPLE: IS DEMOCRACY COMPATIBLE WITH SUCH AN IMBALANCE OF WEALTH AND POWER? WHAT OPPORTUNITIES EXIST? AND FOR WHOM? HOW FREE IS THE "FREE WORKER"?

LOOK OUT! HERE COMES THE "INVISIBLE HAND" OF THE MARKET AGAIN!

THIS VOLUME TELLS THE STORY OF HOW AMERICAN DEMOCRACY CAME TO TERMS WITH THE MODERN INDUSTRIAL STATE. WE'LL LOOK AT:

THE SOUTH ADJUSTING

•

BUSINESS BOOMING AND GOING BUST

•

WORKERS', FARMERS', WOMEN'S, AND BLACK MOVEMENTS MOVING

•

AMERICA EXPANDING

•

COMMUNISM RISING

•

VALUES & MORES ROCKING AND ROLLING

•

SPUTNIKS, BEATNIKS, PEACENIKS, HIPPIES, YIPPIES, & YUPPIES DOING THEIR THING

•

AND LAST, BUT HARDLY LEAST...

CHAPTER 1
DESTRUCTION AND RECONSTRUCTION

THE CIVIL WAR WAS DEVASTATING: FOUR YEARS OF CARNAGE... BILLIONS OF DOLLARS DEVOTED TO DESTRUCTION... A MILLION MEN DEAD... THE COUNTRYSIDE LAID WASTE...

BUT MOST OF THE KILLING AND WASTING TOOK PLACE ON ONE SIDE OF THE MASON-DIXON LINE: THE SOUTHERN SIDE.

8

MEANWHILE, THE NORTH WAS ALL HUSTLE AND BUSTLE: 900,000 IMMIGRANTS HAD MORE THAN REPLACED THE WAR DEAD.

WAR CONTRACTS HAD FATTENED INDUSTRY... WESTWARD EXPANSION PROCEEDED AS USUAL, AND A TRANSCONTINENTAL RAILROAD WAS UNDER CONSTRUCTION.

WAR? WHAT WAR?

I SAY, LET'S BUILD A TOWER UNTO HEAVEN.

VOT?

POSSIBLY IRRELEVANT BIBLICAL REFERENCE →

UP IN WASHINGTON,
THE REPUBLICAN-
DOMINATED GOVERNMENT
PONDERED THE PROBLEM
OF THE SOUTH: HOW
TO PUT THE SOUTH
TOGETHER AGAIN?
AND HOW TO DO IT
DIFFERENTLY FROM
THE LAST TIME?

ABOVE ALL,
GENTLEMEN,
HOW DO WE
MAKE IT VOTE
REPUBLICAN??

WITH
MALICE
TOWARDS
NONE...

BEFORE THE
WAR'S END,
PRES. LINCOLN
SUGGESTED A MILD
"TEN PERCENT
SOLUTION."

ANY SECEDED
STATE WHERE
10% OF THE
ELECTORATE
SWORE A LOYALTY
OATH COULD
FORM A STATE
GOVERNMENT
AND RETURN
TO THE GOOD,
OLD U.S.A.

WOKE UP THIS MORNIN',
BLUES ALL 'ROUND MY HEAD...
WITH THAT 10% SOLUTION,
MIGHT AS WELL STAY IN BED...

HIS SUCCESSOR, ANDREW
JOHNSON, CONTINUED THIS
POLICY, WHICH IN EFFECT
ALLOWED THE LOYAL WHITES
TO REBUILD THE SOUTH,
WITHOUT BLACK PARTICIPATION.

10

IN SEVERAL SOUTHERN STATES, 10% SWIFTLY SWORE LOYALTY!

THEY FORMED NEW GOVERNMENTS, HELD ELECTIONS, AND TURNED TO THE USUAL POLITICIANS FOR LEADERSHIP. SO THE SOUTHERN DELEGATES TO THE 1866 CONGRESS INCLUDED NUMEROUS FORMER CONFEDERATE OFFICIALS.

THE REPUBLICAN CONGRESS SLAMMED THE DOOR ON THE "DIXIECRATS."

...WHICH BRINGS US TO THE EVENTFUL YEAR

WOTTA YEAR!

IT BEGAN WITH CONGRESSIONAL HEARINGS ON CONDITIONS IN THE SOUTH... AND WHAT CONGRESS HEARD WAS HAIR-RAISING (EXCEPT IN THE CASE OF REP. THADDEUS STEVENS, WHO WORE A WIG).

ALTHOUGH THE CONFEDERACY HAD SUFFERED MILITARY DEFEAT, CONGRESS WAS TOLD, THE SPIRIT OF THE OLD SOUTH LIVED ON!

BAILIFF!! ARREST THAT GHOST!!

12

DESPITE EMANCIPATION, THE WHITE SOUTH WAS DOING ITS UTMOST TO KEEP BLACKS "IN THEIR PLACE."

WHUT PLACE IS THAT?

ANY PLACE A WHITE MAN WON'T GO...

THE NEW SOUTHERN GOVERNMENTS ALL PASSED "BLACK CODES", SPECIAL REGULATIONS JUST FOR BLACK PEOPLE.

I DON'T LIKE THE SMELL OF THIS...

FOR EXAMPLE:

* NO BLACK COULD OWN A BUSINESS

* ALL BLACKS HAD TO SIGN A 1-YEAR LABOR CONTRACT— WAGES PAYABLE AT YEAR'S END

* NO BLACK COULD TRAVEL WITHOUT PERMISSION

* FLOGGING FOR BLACK VAGRANTS

* BLACK FELONS TO BE "SOLD" INTO SERVICE TO A "MASTER"

* NO VOTE, JURY DUTY, OR TESTIMONY IN COURT FOR ANY BLACK...

I'D SAY WE WERE SECOND-CLASS CITIZENS, BUT I'M NOT SURE WE'RE CITIZENS...

AND THAT WASN'T ALL.
IN DECEMBER, 1865, THE
KU KLUX KLAN WAS BORN.
THE KLAN AND OTHER GANGS
TERRORIZED BLACKS ACROSS
THE SOUTH, COMMITTING
MORE THAN ONE MURDER
A DAY IN LOUISIANA
ALONE. AND THE CHANCES
OF BRINGING A
KLANSMAN TO JUSTICE-?

THIS *IS* SOUTHERN JUSTICE!

OH, PARDON ME, BRUHTHUH!

ON MAY 1, IN
MEMPHIS, TENNESSEE,
A BLACK SOLDIER
TRIPPED A WHITE
POLICEMAN.

THE MEMPHIS POLICE DEPARTMENT
ATTACKED THE ARMY BASE.
AFTER A SHOOTOUT (6 DEAD),
THE POLICE TURNED AGAINST
A SOUTH MEMPHIS NEIGHBORHOOD,
AND BY THE TIME THE
INCIDENT ENDED, 46 BLACKS
LAY DEAD, AND 90 SHACKS
AND 12 SCHOOLS HAD BEEN
DESTROYED.

14

TO THE HORRIFIED
MEMBERS OF CONGRESS,
IT SOUNDED AS IF
THE SOUTH WANTED
TO TURN BACK THE
CLOCK TO A
PRE-WAR SETTING!

THEY
DON'T EVEN
KNOW WHAT
TIME IT
IS!

SO CONGRESS — WHICH WAS STILL AN ALL-NORTHERN CONGRESS,
MOSTLY REPUBLICAN — BEGAN DEVISING WAYS TO PROTECT
THE BLACKS AND TO KEEP THE OLD SOUTH'S MENTALITY
OUT OF THE NEW SOUTH.

REP.
BENJAMIN
BUTLER

REP.
THADDEUS
STEVENS

DAMYANKS!

SEN. CHARLES
SUMNER

REP. BENJAMIN
WADE

FOR THIS, THE REPUBLICANS
WERE HATED IN THE
SOUTH FOR GENERATIONS
AFTERWARD!

SOMEONE SUGGESTED
GIVING BLACKS THE
PLANTATIONS THEY
USED TO WORK.
THIS IDEA WAS REJECTED
AS TOO SOCIALISTIC.

THERE WAS ALSO A LIVELY
DEBATE ON ALLOWING THE
BLACKS TO VOTE. SOME
OBJECTED THAT IT WAS
TOO SOON, THAT THE
EX-SLAVES WERE TOO
IGNORANT, THAT THEY
HAD TOO LITTLE
POLITICAL EXPERIENCE.

ON THE OTHER HAND, THESE POINTS WERE MADE:

* THERE WERE PLENTY OF
  IGNORANT WHITE VOTERS

* BLACKS WERE NOT
  IGNORANT OF THEIR
  OWN INTERESTS

* THERE MIGHT NOT BE
  ANOTHER CHANCE TO EXTEND
  THE FRANCHISE TO BLACKS

* EVERY BLACK VOTER
  WOULD BE A REPUBLICAN
  VOTER !!

ACTUALLY, THAT DIDN'T QUITE CLINCH IT YET... THE IDEA OF BLACK SUFFRAGE WAS STILL TOO UNPOPULAR, NORTH AND SOUTH. SOME NORTHERN STATES, LIKE ILLINOIS, EVEN BARRED BLACKS FROM MOVING THERE, MUCH LESS VOTING!

AND THIS OVER HERE IS MISTER LINCOLN'S HOUSE...

BUT CONGRESS WENT MORE THAN HALFWAY WITH A BIG CONSTITUTIONAL AMENDMENT, THE

XIVth.

THE 14TH AMENDMENT, WHILE NOT ACTUALLY GRANTING BLACK SUFFRAGE, DOES REDUCE THE REPRESENTATION IN CONGRESS OF ANY STATE THAT DENIES IT. FURTHERMORE, THE GLORIOUS 14TH STATES FOR THE FIRST TIME THAT BLACKS ARE, IN FACT, CITIZENS, AND THAT—

No state shall make or enforce any law which shall abridge the privileges or immunities of citizens of the United States; nor shall any State deprive any person of life, liberty, or property, without due process of law; nor deny to any person within its jurisdiction the equal protection of the laws.

AMAZING THAT NO ONE THOUGHT OF THIS BEFORE!

CONGRESS NOW
DELIVERED THE
SOUTH AN ULTIMATUM:
RATIFY THE 14TH
AMENDMENT, OR ELSE.
THIS THE SOUTH WAS
UNWILLING TO DO.

A FURTHER OBSTACLE WAS
NONE OTHER THAN PRESIDENT
ANDREW JOHNSON,
WHO URGED SOUTHERNERS TO RESIST
THE CONGRESSIONAL "ASSASSINS."
A TENNESSEE DEMOCRAT WHO
HAD REMAINED LOYAL TO THE
UNION, A POOR WHITE WHO
HATED SOUTHERN ARISTOCRATS
ABOUT EQUALLY TO BLACKS,
JOHNSON HAD DECIDED THAT
THE CIVIL WAR WAS HISTORY,
ITS ISSUES SETTLED.

IN JULY CAME THE NEXT MASSACRE, WHEN POLICE LED AN
ATTACK ON A REPUBLICAN PARTY CONVENTION IN NEW ORLEANS.
ONE RIOTER'S CRY WAS:

As the congressional elections approached, the president accused the republicans of plotting a black uprising and the overthrow of the constitution!

His wild campaign speeches divided the electorate...

When the elections were over, the republicans were stronger than ever, controlling ⅔ of both houses of congress!!

AND SO, 1866 FINALLY PASSED INTO

1867.

VETO!

VETO!

VETO!

OVER PRESIDENT JOHNSON'S
REPEATED VETOES, CONGRESS
PASSED ITS OWN TOUGH
RECONSTRUCTION PLAN, WHICH
REQUIRED THE SOUTHERN
STATES TO ——————

* CONTINUE UNDER MILITARY
  OCCUPATION BY THE
  UNION ARMY

* WRITE NEW STATE
  CONSTITUTIONS
  GUARANTEEING EQUAL
  RIGHTS TO BLACKS

* GIVE THE VOTE TO BLACKS

* RATIFY THE
  14TH AMENDMENT

NOW
CONGRESS
CALLS THE
TUNE!

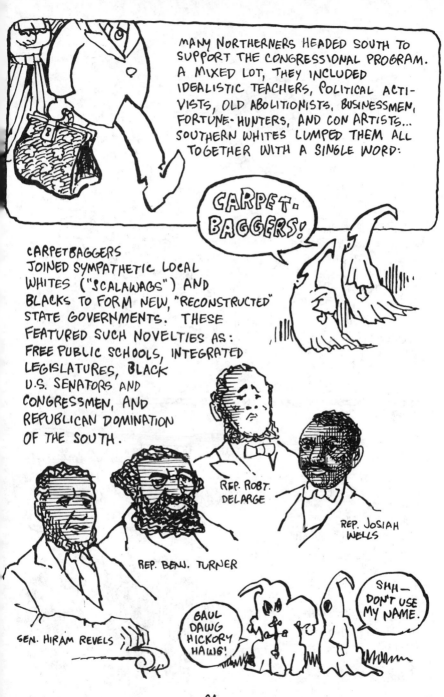

MANY NORTHERNERS HEADED SOUTH TO SUPPORT THE CONGRESSIONAL PROGRAM. A MIXED LOT, THEY INCLUDED IDEALISTIC TEACHERS, POLITICAL ACTIVISTS, OLD ABOLITIONISTS, BUSINESSMEN, FORTUNE-HUNTERS, AND CON ARTISTS... SOUTHERN WHITES LUMPED THEM ALL TOGETHER WITH A SINGLE WORD:

CARPET-BAGGERS!

CARPETBAGGERS JOINED SYMPATHETIC LOCAL WHITES ("SCALAWAGS") AND BLACKS TO FORM NEW, "RECONSTRUCTED" STATE GOVERNMENTS. THESE FEATURED SUCH NOVELTIES AS: FREE PUBLIC SCHOOLS, INTEGRATED LEGISLATURES, BLACK U.S. SENATORS AND CONGRESSMEN, AND REPUBLICAN DOMINATION OF THE SOUTH.

REP. ROBT. DELARGE

REP. JOSIAH WELLS

REP. BEN. TURNER

SEN. HIRAM REVELS

GAUL DAWG HICKORY HAWG!

SHH— DON'T USE MY NAME.

21

ALSO IN 1867, CONGRESS AND PRESIDENT BROKE BRIEFLY FROM BICKERING TO AGREE ON THE PURCHASE OF **ALASKA** FROM RUSSIA. (IMAGINE IF IT WERE STILL RUSSIAN!)

QUIVER TREMBLE SHIVER CHATTER

THEN, JUST TO PROVE THAT IT STILL HATED HIM FOR OBSTRUCTING RECONSTRUCTION, THE HOUSE OF REPRESENTATIVES **impeached** PRES. JOHNSON... BUT THE SENATE ACQUITTED HIM, ON THE GROUNDS THAT BEING OBNOXIOUS WAS NEITHER A HIGH CRIME NOR A MISDEMEANOR.

WHEW!

WHAT WOULD BE HIGH CRIME, IN CASE WE DO THIS AGAIN?

OH... BREAKING AND ENTERING, SAY...

OH, COME **ON!** WHAT PRESIDENT WOULD EVER BE GUILTY OF **THAT**?!

22

THE WHOLE IMPEACHMENT
EXERCISE WAS SILLY...
JOHNSON WOULD BE OUT
OF OFFICE IN A FEW MONTHS,
ANYWAY, AS THE REPUBLICAN
CANDIDATE, WAR HERO

ULYSSES S. GRANT,

SQUEAKED INTO THE
PRESIDENCY IN 1868
(THANKS ENTIRELY TO
BLACK VOTES IN THE
SOUTH, BY THE WAY).

WITH GRANT IN THE
WHITE HOUSE, THE
REPUBLICAN CONGRESS
PASSED THE

XVth AMENDMENT,

WHICH FINALLY GAVE THE VOTE TO ALL BLACK MEN.

(UNTIL THEN,
PARADOXICALLY,
BLACKS COULD VOTE
IN THE SOUTH,
WHICH WAS CONTROLLED
BY THE FEDS,
BUT NOT IN THE
NORTH, WHERE
VOTING QUALIFICATIONS
WERE DECIDED BY THE
INDIVIDUAL STATES.)

HALLEY-
LOO-YAH!
NOW I DON'T
HAVE TO MOVE
BACK TO
MISSISSIPPI!

UNTIL 1877, THE SOUTH
LIVED UNDER RECONSTRUCTION
GOVERNMENTS. THESE YEARS
HAVE BECOME THE SUBJECT
OF A POPULAR MYTH, "THE
EVILS OF RECONSTRUCTION."
THIS MYTH, WHILE NOT
ENTIRELY FALSE, WAS NOT
ENTIRELY TRUE, EITHER.

HERE ARE SOME

RECONSTRUCTION MYTHS & REALITIES:

MYTH: SOUTHERN WHITES WERE DISENFRANCHISED AND RULED OVER BY BLACKS.

HEY! NO FAIR! REALITY USES MORE WORDS THAN MYTH!

MYTH: THE BLACK LEGISLATORS WERE IGNORANT BUFFOONS WHO LOOKED RIDICULOUS "PLAYING AT GOVERNMENT."

REALITY: ALTHOUGH PARTICIPANTS IN THE REBELLION WERE DISENFRANCHISED, THE NEW STATE CONSTITUTIONS, WHICH ABOLISHED PROPERTY QUALIFICATIONS FOR VOTERS, ACTUALLY ENFRANCHISED MILLIONS OF WHITES FOR THE FIRST TIME.

AND WE VOTED!

REALITY: WHILE SOME OF THEM WERE FRESH FROM THE FARM, MANY OTHERS WERE WELL-EDUCATED ANTI-SLAVERY ACTIVISTS.

RIDICULE IS IN THE MOUTH OF THE BEHOLDER!

MYTH: THE BLACKS WERE TOOLS OF NORTHERN "CARPETBAGGERS," DRIVEN BY GREED AND REVENGE.

REALITY: MANY CARPET-BAGGERS WERE IDEALISTIC REFORMERS, COOPERATING WITH BLACKS ON SUCH PROGRAMS AS: EXTENDING DEMOCRACY TO POOR WHITES _AND_ BLACKS; REFORMING THE PENAL SYSTEM; RESTORING THE ECONOMY; AND BUILDING THE SOUTH'S FIRST PUBLIC SCHOOL SYSTEM.

MYTH: "HEEDLESS" SPENDING DROVE THE SOUTHERN GOVERNMENTS DEEP INTO DEBT.

REALITY: THE TAX BASE HAD BEEN DESTROYED BY WAR. URGENTLY NEEDED PROGRAMS OF EDUCATION AND ECONOMIC DEVELOPMENT HAD TO BE FINANCED BY BORROWING.

MYTH: THE KU KLUX KLAN WAS NECESSARY TO RESTORE THE HONOR OF THE WHITE RACE.

REALITY: SOME PEOPLE HAVE A FUNNY IDEA OF HONOR.

MYTH: THE RECONSTRUCTION GOVERNMENTS WERE NOTHING BUT A "SATURNALIA OF CORRUPTION."

TO QUOTE THE ENCYCLOPAEDIA BRITANNICA!

REALITY: THERE WAS, IN FACT, WIDESPREAD CORRUPTION. HOWEVER, IT IS HARDLY FAIR TO SINGLE OUT THE SOUTH HERE, BECAUSE IN THE 1870's, CORRUPTION HAD BECOME THE NATIONAL PASTIME! READ ON...

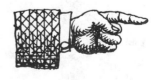

CHAPTER 2
◇ WHERE THE RAILROADS ROAM ◇

IN 1866 (OR WAS IT 1867?*), THE FLAMBOYANT, YOUNG **WILLIAM F. CODY** SIGNED A CONTRACT TO PROVIDE BISON MEAT TO THE CONSTRUCTION WORKERS OF THE KANSAS PACIFIC RAILWAY.

I DON'T LIKE THE SOUND OF THIS...

CODY WAS NO MEAT PACKER... HE PACKED A GUN INSTEAD (NICKNAMED "LUCRETIA BORGIA"). HIS PLAN WAS TO RUSTLE UP GRUB WHERE HE FOUND IT... BECAUSE THE KANSAS PLAINS WERE A VERITABLE LIVING MEAT LOCKER, WITH BISON AS FAR AS THE EYE COULD SEE!

MOVE OVER!

IT'S GOOD TO BE DEEP IN THE PACK!

WHAT THE HECK ARE WE RUNNING FROM? I CAN'T SEE A THING!

* ACCURATE INFORMATION ABOUT BILL CODY IS HARD TO COME BY. HE PERSONALLY INVENTED ENOUGH INACCURACIES TO FILL VOLUMES.

IN EIGHT MONTHS*
CODY BAGGED OVER
4200 BISON AND
EARNED HIMSELF A
NICKNAME AS WELL:

"BUFFALO
BILL."

THIS WAS JUST THE BEGINNING OF THE GREAT BUFFALO
SLAUGHTER. IT WAS INCREDIBLY WASTEFUL: CODY TOOK
ONLY THE HAMS AND HUMPS, LEAVING THE REST TO THE
HAPPY VULTURES.

EVEN SO, HE
SUPPLIED ENOUGH
MEAT TO FEED
A SMALL ARMY
OF RAILROAD
WORKERS!

*OR EIGHTEEN. SEE PREVIOUS FOOTNOTE.

ALL THOSE WORKERS EATING ALL THOSE BUFFALO WAS A CLEAR SIGN THAT THE RAILROAD BUSINESS WAS BOOMING. IN THE 1860's, RAILROAD BARONS' FORTUNES WERE RISING EVEN FASTER THAN THE BUFFALO POPULATION WAS FALLING.

THE BOOM HAD ACTUALLY BEGUN WITH THE CIVIL WAR, WHEN CONGRESS HATCHED A TRULY GRAND SCHEME: BUILD A TRANSCONTINENTAL RAILWAY.

BUT A PROJECT SO ENORMOUS HAD SCARCELY BEEN IMAGINED BEFORE! WHO COULD POSSIBLY AFFORD IT? SUCH A HUGE INVESTMENT IN LAND, LABOR, AND EQUIPMENT WAS BEYOND THE ABILITY OF ANY PRIVATE COMPANY.

IT WAS SUGGESTED THAT THE GOVERNMENT ITSELF COULD BUILD AND RUN THE GREAT RAILROAD — BUT NO, THAT WOULD BE SOCIALISTIC!

SO THE GOVERNMENT CAME UP WITH A BRILLIANT SOLUTION: SIMPLY **GIVE** THE LAND AND LEND THE MONEY TO PRIVATE RAILROAD COMPANIES! THE AMOUNT OF LAND EVENTUALLY HANDED OVER WAS INCREDIBLE: MORE THAN 200 MILLION ACRES!!

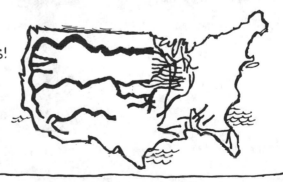

AND WHO WERE THESE RAILROAD COMPANIES? WELL, IN THOSE DAYS, WHEN THE INDUSTRY WAS YOUNG, ANYONE WHO **SAID** HE WAS A RAILROAD COULD **BE** A RAILROAD. AND WITH SUCH HIGH STAKES, THERE WERE MANY CONTENDERS!!

FOR EXAMPLE, FOUR CALIFORNIA SHOPKEEPERS, ARMED WITH SOME ENGINEERING SURVEYS, DECLARED THEMSELVES THE **CENTRAL PACIFIC** RAILROAD. ONE OF THEM HEADED TO WASHINGTON WITH A SUITCASE FULL OF CASH...

...AND "PERSUADED" CONGRESS TO GIVE THE WESTERN END OF THE TRANSCONTINENTAL PROJECT TO HIMSELF AND HIS PARTNERS. PRACTICALLY OVERNIGHT, THEIR FORTUNES MULTIPLIED FROM THE TENS OF THOUSANDS TO THE TENS OF MILLIONS. THEY WERE NOW A RAILROAD!!

HOPKINS   CROCKER   STANFORD   HUNTINGTON

THE EASTERN HALF OF THE ROUTE WAS ASSIGNED TO THE

UNION PACIFIC

COMPANY. DESPITE THE PATRIOTIC NAME, THE CORPORATION'S DIRECTORS FOUND A WAY TO MILK CONGRESS FOR MILLIONS OF DOLLARS...

THE SCHEME WAS SIMPLE: THEY HIRED A FIRM NAMED *CREDIT MOBILIER* TO DO THE CONSTRUCTION WORK, THEN OVERPAID CREDIT MOBILIER BY AN ENORMOUS FACTOR.

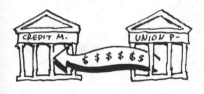

THE BEAUTY OF IT WAS THAT THE OWNERS OF CREDIT MOBILIER AND THE OWNERS OF THE UNION PACIFIC WERE — THE VERY SAME PEOPLE!!

ALTHOUGH MILLIONS IN PUBLIC FUNDS DISAPPEARED INTO THE RAILROADERS' BANK ACCOUNTS, CONGRESS WAS SILENT —

AND NO WONDER: THE UNION PACIFIC MEN HAD BESTOWED MANY SHARES OF PROFITABLE STOCK UPON THE COMPLIANT CONGRESSPEOPLE!

RAILROADERS WEREN'T THE ONLY ONES WHO MULTIPLIED THEIR MONEY IN THE CIVIL WAR.

SEVERAL OF AMERICA'S MOST FAMOUS FORTUNES DATE FROM THE 1860'S!

FOR INSTANCE (L. TO R.): JOHN D. ROCKEFELLER (OIL), PHILIP ARMOUR (MEAT), ANDREW CARNEGIE (IRON & STEEL), J.P. MORGAN (BANKING) — ALL WERE MEN IN THEIR 20'S DURING THE CIVIL WAR, AND ALL CHOSE BUSINESS OVER BATTLE!

"I HAD HOPED MY BOY WAS GOING TO MAKE A SMART, INTELLIGENT BUSINESSMAN, AND WAS NOT SUCH A GOOSE AS TO BE SEDUCED FROM DUTY [SIC] BY THE DECLAMATIONS OF BUNCOMBED SPEECHES. IT IS ONLY GREENHORNS WHO ENLIST... A MAN MAY BE A PATRIOT WITHOUT RISKING HIS OWN LIFE... THERE ARE PLENTY OF OTHER LIVES LESS VALUABLE..."

— JUDGE THOMAS MELLON TO HIS SON

"I'M RICH! I'M RICH!"
— ANDREW CARNEGIE

"WE COULD NOT BE EXPECTED TO LEAVE OUR COMFORTABLE HOMES WITHOUT SOME GREAT INDUCEMENT."
— BANKER JAY COOKE

"YOU CAN SELL ANYTHING TO THE GOVERNMENT AT ANY PRICE IF YOU'VE GOT THE NERVE TO ASK."
— JIM FISK

"TO CONTINUE MUCH LONGER WITH MOST OF MY THOUGHTS WHOLLY UPON THE WAY TO MAKE MONEY IN THE SHORTEST TIME MUST DEGRADE ME BEYOND HOPE OF PERMANENT RECOVERY."
— ANDREW CARNEGIE

"I LIKE TO TURN BRISTLES, BLOOD, BONES, AND THE INSIDES AND OUTSIDES OF PIGS AND BULLOCKS INTO REVENUE." — P. ARMOUR

AS THEIR BUSINESSES
BOOMED, THESE
GENIUSES OF HIGH
FINANCE INVENTED
NEW, FABULOUS,
AND NOT ALWAYS
HONEST METHODS
OF MANIPULATING
MONEY. FOR SOME
REASON, THESE ARE
OFTEN DESCRIBED
IN LIQUID METAPHORS,

SUCH AS:

STOCK WATERING

SIPHONING PROCEEDS

SKIMMING ASSETS

FLOODING MARKETS

MILKING COMPANIES

FLOATING LOANS

SINKING FUNDS

POOLS

FINANCIAL RESERVOIRS

(NOTE: "LAUNDERING"
MONEY WASN'T
INVENTED UNTIL
LATER.)

35

AMERICANS ADMIRED THE WITS, ENERGY, AND EVEN THE
RUTHLESSNESS OF THESE CORSAIRS. AFTER ALL, WASN'T
COMPETITION PART OF THE NATURAL ORDER? WASN'T
SUCCESS THE SURVIVAL OF THE FITTEST?
IT WAS PRIMAL! IT WAS
DARWINIAN!*

> GEE! I
> WISH I'D
> THOUGHT
> OF THAT!

IN THIS ECONOMIC
STRUGGLE FOR EXISTENCE,
THE POST-WAR
CAPITALISTS OFTEN
DISPLAYED THE BUSINESS
ETHICS OF A
CHIMPANZEE.

*DARWIN'S *THE ORIGIN OF SPECIES* APPEARED IN 1859.

36

THEY "PURCHASED" REPRESENTATIVES, SENATORS, THE PRESIDENT'S BROTHER-IN-LAW... EVERY INDUSTRY HAD GOVERNMENT OFFICIALS IN ITS POCKET... IN CALIFORNIA, THE RAILROAD EVEN TOSSED GOLD COINS TO THE VOTERS ON ELECTION DAY!

OOPS!

IN THE JARGON OF THE TIME, A CORRUPT NETWORK WAS A "RING." THERE WAS A WHISKEY RING, AN ERIE RAILROAD RING, THE CREDIT MOBILIER RING, A GOLD RING, A U.S. CUSTOMS RING, A CANAL RING, A MILWAUKEE RING, N.Y.'S "BOSS" TWEED RING, AND COUNTLESS OTHER STATE, COUNTY, AND MUNICIPAL RINGS.

EVERYTHING BUT A BATHTUB RING!

(AND OF COURSE, SOME OF THESE RINGS REACHED INTO THE RECONSTRUCTION SOUTH, GIVING THE RACISTS A NEW EXCUSE TO QUESTION THE BLACKS' "CAPACITY" FOR HONEST GOVERNMENT.)

MY BAG'S CAPACITY IS DEFINITELY BIGGER...

37

AND NOW, BACK TO BUFFALO BILL COUNTRY:

IN 1875, COL.
GEORGE ARMSTRONG
CUSTER, WITH
HIS DOGS, LED AN
EXPLORING PARTY
INTO DAKOTA'S
BLACK HILLS,
LOOKING FOR
GOLD. THIS WAS
INDIAN COUNTRY,
GUARANTEED BY
SOLEMN TREATY.

CUSTER WAS FOLLOWED, AS SOON AS WORD GOT OUT, BY ANOTHER
INVASION OF PROSPECTORS, SPECULATORS, HARDWARE SALESMEN,
MULES, TEAMSTERS, CLAIM-JUMPERS, COOKS, LAUNDRESSES, AND
CAMP-FOLLOWERS.

(IT WAS GOVERNMENT POLICY
TO "DISAPPROVE" OF THIS
ONSLAUGHT, WHILE DOING
NOTHING TO STOP IT...)

GOLD!!
IT'S NATURE'S
LOTTERY!

BY THIS TIME, THE PLAINS INDIANS WERE ALREADY THREATENED BY THE DWINDLING SUPPLY OF BUFFALO.

THE GOVERNMENT URGED THE SIOUX AND CHEYENNE TO GIVE UP THEIR HOME ON THE RANGE FOR A BUNK ON THE RESERVATION... TO EXCHANGE BUFFALO ROBES FOR WOOL BLANKETS, AND BUFFALO JERKY FOR RESERVATION BEEF.

BUT NOW, WITH THE FRESH INVASION OF WHITE SETTLERS, THE INDIANS WENT ON THE WARPATH!

DESPITE THE HOSTILITIES, OFFICIAL GOVERNMENT RECORDS SHOWED THAT NEARLY ALL OF THE PLAINS INDIANS WERE SAFELY ON THE RESERVATIONS.

BUT, IN AN AGE OF CORRUPTION, THE RECORDS WERE FALSIFIED BY CORRUPT GOVERNMENT AGENTS. THE AGENTS, IN CHARGE OF THE RESERVATIONS, RECEIVED FUNDS ACCORDING TO THE NUMBER OF "THEIR" INDIANS. THIS NUMBER THEY ROUTINELY INFLATED, SKIMMING OFF THE MONEY OF THOUSANDS OF IMAGINARY OR ABSENT SOULS.

RESERVATION	OFFICIAL POPULATION	ACTUAL POPULATION
SPOTTED TAIL	9,610	2,315
RED CLOUD	12,873	4,760
CHEYENNE RIVER	7,586	2,280
STANDING ROCK	7,322	2,305

ADDING UP THE NUMBERS, YOU GET A DISCREPANCY OF ROUGHLY 25,000...

... MOST OF WHOM WERE CAMPED ALONG THE BANKS OF THE LITTLE BIG HORN RIVER, MONTANA, WHEN COL. CUSTER'S CAVALRY ARRIVED ON A SEARCH-AND-DESTROY MISSION (JUNE 25, 1876).

CUSTER, RECEIVING THE SURPRISE OF HIS LIFE, MADE A LAST STAND. ABOUT 265 CAVALRYMEN FELL THAT DAY — VICTIMS OF GOVERNMENT CORRUPTION!

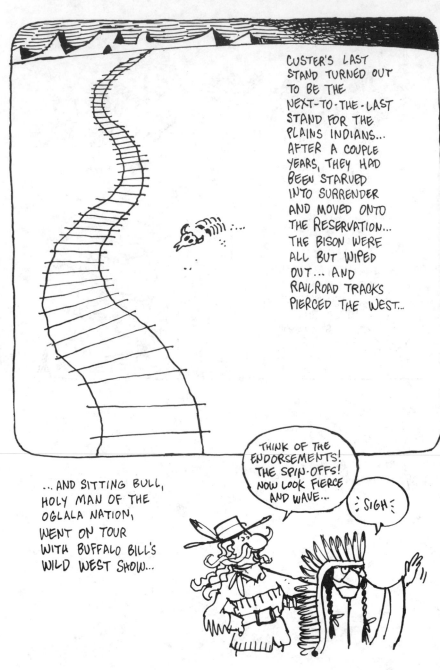

CUSTER'S LAST STAND TURNED OUT TO BE THE NEXT-TO-THE-LAST STAND FOR THE PLAINS INDIANS... AFTER A COUPLE YEARS, THEY HAD BEEN STARVED INTO SURRENDER AND MOVED ONTO THE RESERVATION... THE BISON WERE ALL BUT WIPED OUT... AND RAILROAD TRACKS PIERCED THE WEST...

...AND SITTING BULL, HOLY MAN OF THE OGLALA NATION, WENT ON TOUR WITH BUFFALO BILL'S WILD WEST SHOW...

THINK OF THE ENDORSEMENTS! THE SPIN-OFFS! NOW LOOK FIERCE AND WAVE...

:SIGH:

42

···◇ CHAPTER 3 ◇···
LABOR PAINS

JULY 4, 1876, WAS THE UNITED STATES' HUNDREDTH BIRTHDAY.

IN THE GRAND AMERICAN TRADITION, THE NATION THREW A NOISY PARTY, WITH RINGING SPEECHES, BOOMING BELLS, BLASTING BRASS BANDS, AND EAR-INJURING FIREWORKS.

BUT THE CELEBRATION WAS A GLOOMY ONE FOR PRESIDENT GRANT AND THE REPUBLICANS.

1876 WAS ALSO AN ELECTION YEAR, AND IT LOOKED BAD FOR THE PARTY THAT GAVE US THE MOST CORRUPT ADMINISTRATION IN THE REPUBLIC'S HISTORY...

FOR PRESIDENT THE DEMOCRATS RAN A "REFORM" CANDIDATE, SAMUEL **TILDEN**, WHILE THE REPUBLICANS NOMINATED THE BUSINESS-AND-BEARDS-AS-USUAL RUTHERFORD B. **HAYES**. THE RESULT WAS SURPRISING...

AT FIRST, TILDEN SEEMED TO HAVE WON EASILY. BUT THE REPUBLICANS CHALLENGED HIS VOTES IN FOUR STATES, AND PRODUCED ALTERNATIVE RETURNS FAVORING HAYES.

THEY ACCUSED THE DEMOCRATS OF INTIMIDATING BLACK VOTERS WITH KU KLUX KLAN TACTICS, WHILE THE DEMOCRATS CHARGED THE REPUBLICANS WITH BUYING VOTES.

BOTH WERE CORRECT!

THE GOVERNMENT STOPPED DEAD ON THE ISSUE. CONGRESSIONAL DEBATE GAVE WAY TO SHOUTING, THEN SCREAMING, AND FINALLY A HIGH WHINE.

SOUNDS LIKE THE CIVIL WAR STARTING AGAIN...

A COMMISSION OF 8 REPUBLICANS AND 7 DEMOCRATS WAS APPOINTED TO RESOLVE THE IMPASSE. IT VOTED, 8-7, IN FAVOR OF HAYES.

SURPRISE!

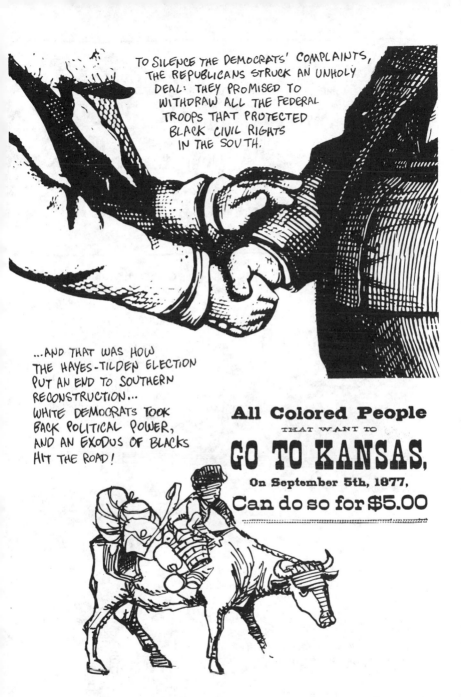

TO SILENCE THE DEMOCRATS' COMPLAINTS, THE REPUBLICANS STRUCK AN UNHOLY DEAL: THEY PROMISED TO WITHDRAW ALL THE FEDERAL TROOPS THAT PROTECTED BLACK CIVIL RIGHTS IN THE SOUTH.

...AND THAT WAS HOW THE HAYES-TILDEN ELECTION PUT AN END TO SOUTHERN RECONSTRUCTION... WHITE DEMOCRATS TOOK BACK POLITICAL POWER, AND AN EXODUS OF BLACKS HIT THE ROAD!

All Colored People
THAT WANT TO
GO TO KANSAS,
On September 5th, 1877,
Can do so for **$5.00**

THE REPUBLICANS HAD SCARCELY FINISHED EXHALING THEIR SIGH OF RELIEF WHEN THE NATION WAS ROCKED BY SOMETHING CALLED ⇨

THE GREAT UPHEAVAL

OF 1877...

THIS UNDER-REPORTED HISTORICAL EPISODE BEGAN IN PENNSYLVANIA WITH A STRIKE AGAINST THE B&O RAILROAD. IN PITTSBURGH, TROOPS ATTACKED THE STRIKERS, KILLING 20. THE INFURIATED WORKERS SEIZED THE TRAIN YARDS AND TORCHED THE ROUNDHOUSE.

THE STRIKE SPREAD TO SANDUSKY, BUFFALO, MILWAUKEE, CLEVELAND, ST. LOUIS. EVERYWHERE, CROWDS GATHERED TO SUPPORT THE STRIKERS, WHILE POLICE AND GUARDSMEN BACKED OFF — OR JOINED THE MOB THEMSELVES!!

I'M JUST A WORKER IN A BLUE SUIT!

SOON THE WORKERS WERE MANAGING THE RAILROADS THEMSELVES, MOVING STRIKE LEADERS AND INFORMATION ALMOST AT WILL.

ST. LOUIS FELL BRIEFLY UNDER THE CONTROL OF THE STRIKE COMMITTEE — A SORT OF "WORKERS' SOVIET" — WHICH SHUT DOWN THE CITY WITH A GENERAL STRIKE. RHETORIC GREW REVOLUTIONARY!

THIS MAY BE THE BEGINNING OF A GREAT CIVIL WAR IN THIS COUNTRY, BETWEEN LABOR AND CAPITAL... IT ONLY NEEDS THAT THE STRIKERS SHOULD BOLDLY ATTACK AND ROUT THE TROOPS.

THE WORKING MEN INTEND NOW TO ASSERT THEIR RIGHTS, EVEN IF THE RESULT IS SHEDDING OF BLOOD!

COMMUNISM IMPENDS!

AT LAST, THE NEW PRESIDENT ORDERED IN THE ARMY, WHICH BLOODILY CRUSHED THE STRIKE... THE WORKERS, DESPITE LOSING, WENT BACK TO WORK WITH A SPRING IN THEIR STEP!

A P.S.: AS A DIRECT RESULT OF THE 1877 UPRISING, THE GOVERNMENT NERVOUSLY BUILT THE GREAT STONE ARMORIES YOU SEE IN SO MANY AMERICAN CITIES — NOT AGAINST FOREIGN INVASION, BUT WORKERS' REBELLION!!

47

HOW HAD THIS HAPPENED?? THE GREAT UPHEAVAL HAD SEEMINGLY HEAVED UP FROM NOWHERE! WHO WOULD ATTACK THE SYSTEM IN THIS WAY? WASN'T AMERICAN INDUSTRY A **WONDERFUL** THING???

YOU JUST DON'T APPRECIATE THE **GOOD** IT'S DONE **ALL** OF US!

THAT'S RIGHT!

IN TRUTH, AMERICAN INDUSTRY HAD ITS WONDERFUL POINTS. IN A FEW SHORT YEARS (AND SEVERAL LONG ONES), IT HAD MECHANIZED FARM LIFE WITH LABOR-SAVING DEVICES, CREATED AN AMAZING TRANSPORTATION SYSTEM, AND MASS-PRODUCED CLOTHING, FURNITURE, AND OTHER CONSUMER ITEMS.

THE GOOD LIFE DEPENDS ON IT!

BUT ALAS... THE ECONOMY HAD THIS UNPLEASANT TENDENCY TO

CRASH

WHEN THAT HAPPENED, WORKERS LOST THEIR JOBS, WAGES FELL, BANKRUPTCIES ROSE, AND PEOPLE FOUND THEMSELVES SURROUNDED BY CONSUMER GOODS THEY COULDN'T AFFORD — FOOD, FOR EXAMPLE...

AHEM...

...WHILE ROCKEFELLER AND CARNEGIE ACTUALLY GREW RICHER BY DEVOURING THEIR DISTRESSED COMPETITORS!

YOU SEE? EVERY CLOUD HAS A SILVER LINING!

THE FIRST CRASH
AFTER THE
CIVIL WAR WAS THE

PANIC
OF
1873.

I AM GLAD TO SEE THAT A SYSTEM OF LABOR PREVAILS UNDER WHICH LABORERS MAY STRIKE WHEN THEY WANT TO,

ABE LINCOLN HAD SAID.

AS HARD TIMES DRAGGED ON THROUGH 1873, '74, '75, AND '76, WORKERS' FAMILIES HAD TO LIVE ON CORNBREAD AND BEANS, AND "FREE LABOR" BEGAN SOUNDING LIKE A SLOGAN AS EMPTY AS THEIR STOMACHS.

FREE TO BEEE... WHAT'S LEFT OF MEEE...

THE CIVIL WAR—WASN'T THAT THE WAR TO PROTECT FREE LABOR?

WELL, NOW I'M FREE!

IN 1875, A WAVE OF STRIKES HIT THE COAL MINES (ACCIDENT RATE: 80 DEATHS PER YEAR). MANAGEMENT PULLED OUT ALL THE STOPS: PRIVATE ARMIES OF STRIKEBREAKERS (THE NOTORIOUS PINKERTON "DETECTIVES"), CHARGES OF TERRORISM AGAINST STRIKE LEADERS, ETC.... THIS WAS THE BACKGROUND OF 1877.

I CAN HIRE ONE HALF OF THE WORKING CLASS TO KILL THE OTHER HALF,

SAID INDUSTRIALIST JAY GOULD.

THIS PARTLY ACCOUNTS FOR STRIKERS' MILITANT RHETORIC DURING THE 1877 UPRISING... ANOTHER REASON WAS THE FACT THAT THERE WERE, IN FACT, SOME SOCIALISTS INVOLVED!

RUN! BUT WHICH WAY?

THE SOCIALIST MOVEMENT, IN THE OPINION OF MOST, BEGAN IN **1848**, WHEN A WAVE OF EUROPEAN REVOLUTIONS SPAWNED **KARL MARX**'S *COMMUNIST MANIFESTO.*

BY 1864 MARX HEADED THE INTERNATIONAL WORKING MEN'S ASSOCIATION (WHICH WAS NICKNAMED THE "FIRST INTERNATIONAL" SOMETIME DURING THE ORGANIZATION OF THE SECOND INTERNATIONAL).

BY 1877, AMERICA'S TEEMING IMMIGRANT POPULATION INCLUDED ENOUGH SOCIALISTS (MOSTLY GERMAN) TO FOUND A SMALL BUT VERY LOUD **WORKERS' PARTY** AFFILIATED WITH THE FIRST INTERNATIONAL.

WORKERS WITH BOOKS IN THEIR LUGGAGE?

AS THE SOCIALISTS SAW IT, WORKERS WERE LOCKED IN AN ETERNAL

CLASS STRUGGLE

WITH THE OWNERS OF CAPITAL. (CAPITAL = MONEY, STOCKS, BONDS, FACTORIES, MACHINERY, SHIPS, TRAINS, ETC. ETC. ETC.) WHAT THE WORKER NEEDS IS THE OPPOSITE OF WHAT CAPITAL NEEDS.

ACCORDING TO THIS VIEW OF THE WORLD, THE WORKER ALONE CREATES VALUE BY WORKING, WHILE THE CAPITALIST TAKES IT AWAY IN THE FORM OF PROFIT. LOW WAGES, HIGH UNEMPLOYMENT, POLLUTION, UNSAFE FACTORIES ARE NECESSARY FOR PROFITABILITY.* ECONOMIC CRASHES ARE AN INEVITABLE CONSEQUENCE OF THE QUEST FOR PROFIT... AND THE GOVERNMENT, AS STRIKEBREAKER, IS A PURE TOOL OF THE BOSSES...

THE SOCIALISTS' PRESCRIPTION WAS FOR THE WORKERS TO TAKE POLITICAL POWER FROM CAPITAL AND CREATE A WORKERS' STATE. THIS WAS NOW POSSIBLE FOR THE FIRST TIME IN HISTORY, SAID MARX, BECAUSE LARGE-SCALE FACTORIES BROUGHT WORKERS TOGETHER IN INDUSTRIAL ARMIES.

*LOW WAGES, POLLUTION, AND INDUSTRIAL CALAMITIES IN THE PRESENT-DAY SOCIALIST WORLD ARE, OF COURSE, A COMPLETE ACCIDENT THAT DEFIES RATIONAL EXPLANATION.

ON THE OTHER HAND, MOST CAPITALISTS VIEWED THE SOCIALISTS AS LITTLE MORE THAN A GANG OF ALIEN, BOMB-THROWING BANDITTI. NO "REAL" AMERICAN WOULD FOMENT LABOR STRIFE— IT HAD TO BE THE WORK OF FOREIGNERS AND ANARCHIST-SOCIALIST-COMMUNIST AGITATORS!

SMELLS LIKE ROSES

REPUBLICAN BALLOT

DEFERENTIAL YET INTELLIGENT ATTITUDE

HAT IN HAND

"REAL" AMERICAN

SMELLS LIKE GARLIC

HAT COVERS EYES

CRINGING, SHIFTY EXPRESSION

BOMB

CONSPIRATORIAL SLOUCH

UNREAL IMMIGRANT

ALMOST WITHOUT REALIZING IT, THE BOSSES HAD INVENTED

RED·BAITING:

I.E., BREAKING UNIONS BY ATTACKING SOCIALISTS IN THE RANKS.

YOU FOLKS GO RIGHT AHEAD— WE'LL JUST JAIL YOUR PRESIDENT AND IMPUGN YOUR MOTIVES...

52

DESPITE MANAGEMENT'S OPPOSITION, UNION ORGANIZING STEPPED UP AFTER 1877. MOST ACTIVE WERE THE **KNIGHTS OF LABOR,** WHO CONCEALED THEMSELVES FROM THE BOSS WITH SECRET SIGNS AND HANDSHAKES.

AT THE SAME TIME, A YOUNG CIGAR ROLLER NAMED **SAMUEL GOMPERS** HELPED TO FOUND THE **A**MERICAN **F**EDERATION OF **L**ABOR. GOMPERS GUIDED THE AFL AWAY FROM PARTY POLITICS AND INTO A SIMPLE QUEST FOR "MORE" — HIGHER WAGES, SHORTER HOURS, AND BETTER WORKING CONDITIONS. THE AFL'S SKILLED CRAFT UNIONS BECAME AN "ARISTOCRACY OF LABOR."

THE RESURGENT UNION MOVEMENT MADE ITS CAMPAIGN FOR THE '80's A DEMAND FOR AN **8-HOUR DAY.**

NOW THEY WANT TO CHANGE THE COURSE OF THE SUN IN ITS ORBIT!

THE AFL AND OTHERS CALLED FOR A NATIONWIDE DEMONSTRATION: A ONE-DAY **GENERAL STRIKE** ON MAY 1, 1886... A TOTAL WORK STOPPAGE... A ZERO-HOUR DAY FOR THE EIGHT-HOUR DAY.

I'M FOR IT!

THIS EXTREME TACTIC DIVIDED THE MOVEMENT. THE RANK AND FILE GENERALLY FAVORED IT, WHILE THE NERVOUS PRESIDENT OF THE KNIGHTS OF LABOR, **TERENCE POWDERLY**, DISLIKED THE WHOLE IDEA.

ER...
PREMATURE...
JEOPARDIZES OUR GAINS...
COMMUNISTIC...
ETC.
ETC.
ETC.

THE GNAT OF LABOR!

THE DAY ARRIVED... AND ACROSS THE COUNTRY, UNIONISTS GATHERED IN HUGE RALLIES TO HEAR INFLAMMATORY SPEECHES.

Our war-cry is "**DEATH to the foes of the human race!**" *

EVER SINCE THEN, MAY DAY HAS BEEN LABOR DAY — IN EVERY COUNTRY EXCEPT THE UNITED STATES, THAT IS!!

IF THE COMMIES DO IT, WE DON'T!

* FROM A RESOLUTION OF THE ANARCHIST-LED CHICAGO CENTRAL LABOR UNION, 1885.

THE MAY DAY RALLIES WERE PEACEFUL, BUT TWO DAYS LATER, IN CHICAGO, THE POLICE ATTACKED ANOTHER DEMONSTRATION, GENEROUSLY TRYING TO PROTECT THE WORKERS' EARS FROM BECOMING INFLAMED BY THE HOT WORDS, NO DOUBT.

TAKE 2 ASPIRIN AND CALL ME IN THE MORNING.

FIRING INTO THE FLEEING WORKERS' BACKS, THE POLICE KILLED FOUR, AND THE ANARCHIST PRESS SCREAMED BLOODY MURDER, WHICH SEEMED APPROPRIATE.

REVENGE! WORKINGMEN, TO ARMS!... YOU HAVE ENDURED THE MOST ABJECT HUMILIATIONS... WHY? TO SATISFY THE INSATIABLE GREED OF YOUR MASTERS? TO ARMS, WE CALL YOU, TO ARMS!

REVEN[GE]

ON MAY 4, WHILE BREAKING UP YET ANOTHER DEMONSTRATION, SEVEN POLICEMEN WERE KILLED BY A BOMB BLAST — THE HAYMARKET EXPLOSION.

WITHOUT ANY IDEA WHO TOSSED THE BOMB, THE AUTHORITIES ARRESTED — EIGHT ANARCHISTS.

IF THEY AIN'T GUILTY, THEY'RE GONNA BE!!

ALTHOUGH THEIR INVOLVEMENT WAS NEVER PROVED, ONE OF THE PRISONERS SHOWED AT LEAST A PASSING ACQUAINTANCE WITH EXPLOSIVES BY BLOWING HIMSELF UP IN JAIL. FOUR OTHERS WERE HANGED, AND THE REST RECEIVED LONG JAIL SENTENCES.

THE HAYMARKET EVENTS COOLED THE 8-HOUR MOVEMENT, BUT NOT FOR LONG. THE '90'S BROUGHT ANOTHER CRASH AND ANOTHER WAVE OF STRIKES.

WORKERS SEIZED FACTORIES, MINES, TRAIN YARDS PINKERTONS KILLED STRIKERS' FAMILIES... BULLETS FLEW IN SEVERAL DIRECTIONS...

YOU CAN SEE WHY THEY CALL IT "CLASS WAR"!

ONTO THIS WILD STAGE MARCHED THE IMPASSIONED FIGURE OF

EUGENE DEBS,

PRESIDENT OF THE AMERICAN RAILROAD UNION.

IN 1894, THE A R U BACKED A STRIKE AGAINST THE PULLMAN RAILROAD CAR COMPANY.

DEBS WAS AS AMERICAN AS THEY COME:

BORN IN INDIANA...

MARRIED IN THE EPISCOPAL CHURCH

WORKED AS A RAILROAD FIREMAN

ORGANIZED A LOCAL OF THE FIREMEN'S UNION

BECAME ITS NATIONAL SECRETARY-TREASURER

SERVED A TERM IN THE INDIANA LEGISLATURE

HE SHOULD BE PLAYED BY RONALD REAGAN!

THEN, IN 1894, HIS SUPPORT FOR THE PULLMAN STRIKE LANDED HIM IN JAIL. CONVICTED OF OBSTRUCTING THE U.S. MAIL, DEBS AND OTHER UNION OFFICIALS GOT SIX MONTHS, WHICH DEBS PASSED READING MARXIST LITERATURE.

MAYBE SENDING DEBS TO JAIL WASN'T SUCH A GOOD IDEA...

HE EMERGED FROM PRISON A CONVERT TO THE "ALIEN" PHILOSOPHY. THE AMERICAN SOCIALIST MOVEMENT WAS ABOUT TO BECOME AMERICANIZED...

More on Debs next chapter... Now we're looking down on the 1893 Chicago Columbian Exposition, built (a year late) to honor Columbus's 400th anniversary. It's a fitting symbol to end this chapter: the enormous "Palace of Manufactures," covering 30 acres, stuffed with modern industrial wonders: dynamos, telephones, electric motors, automobiles, dynamite, light bulbs, machine guns...

But 18 workers died building this exposition, and hundreds more were injured.

American workers had fought long and hard to improve — or even to maintain — their lot. Here and there they had won victories ... But the 40-hour week, extra pay for overtime work, unemployment insurance, social security, government-enforced safety standards were all still FAR in the future, and working men and women were growing increasingly frustrated.

And not only workers! Many other Americans were tired of the industrial bloodshed... tired of seeing a rich and powerful few drive so many into poverty and debt...

Obviously, something had to be done!! The only question was...

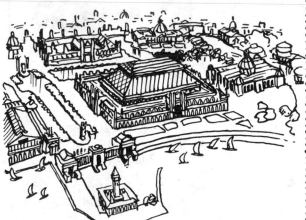

WHAT??

« CHAPTER 4 »

IN WHICH AN AWFUL LOT HAPPENS

Now we enter the final tenth of the nineteenth...

Everything was in flux — electromagnetic flux, that is: electricity powered lamps, streetcars, and elevators in new skyscrapers...

Business was bigger than ever... the lean, mean capitalists of the '70's and '80's were evolving into bloated economic monsters, the TRUSTS.

A **TRUST** WAS SIMPLY A MONOPOLY GOING UNDER AN ANGLO-SAXON NAME...

DURING THE '60's, '70's, AND '80's, BIG COMPANIES HAD USUALLY DEALT WITH SMALLER FRY BY POUNDING THEM INTO THE DUST.

SOMETIMES, THOUGH, IT WAS CHEAPER AND EASIER TO ABSORB COMPETITORS. THE WEAKER COMPANIES WOULD "ENTRUST" THEIR ASSETS TO THE LARGER, IN EXCHANGE FOR CASH OR STOCK, UNTIL ONLY ONE COMPANY WAS LEFT — THE **TRUST.**

STANDARD OIL, UNITED STATES STEEL, GENERAL ELECTRIC, THE BELL SYSTEM, THE COAL TRUST, THE SUGAR TRUST... IN INDUSTRY AFTER INDUSTRY, ONE COMPANY OR SYNDICATE EMERGED TO PLAN STRATEGY, SET PRICES, AND DEAL WITH OTHER TRUSTS.

THIS WAS ALL VERY
RATIONAL, AS ROCKEFELLER
LIKED TO SAY... EXCEPT THAT
THESE MONOPOLIES' POWER NOW
RIVALED THE GOVERNMENT'S!

C'MON!
WHAT GOVERNMENT
HAS POWER LIKE
OURS?

A RAILROAD COULD MAKE OR BREAK WHOLE CITIES AND REGIONS BY
ITS CHOICE OF ROUTE. (THIS IS WHY SEATTLE, WASHINGTON, OUTGREW
NEIGHBORING TACOMA — SEATTLE WAS FAVORED BY THE RAILROAD...
AND MILAN, OHIO, BIRTHPLACE OF THE INVENTOR EDISON, A BOOM TOWN
IN THE DAYS OF CANAL TRAFFIC, WAS BEGGARED WHEN BYPASSED
BY RAIL...)   MONOPOLIES COULD CHARGE WHATEVER THE MARKET
WOULD BEAR, WITHOUT WORRYING ABOUT THE COMPETITION.

COMPETITION
IS
OUTMODED!

ANY THREAT OF
FOREIGN COMPETITION
WAS PREVENTED BY
HIGH TARIFFS ON
IMPORTED GOODS.

AND
THE LOW
ETHICS OF
RENTED
SENATORS!

MEANWHILE, DOWN ON THE FARM, WHERE MOST AMERICANS STILL LIVED, THEY WERE FEELING MONOPOLY'S FULL EXTRACTIVE POWER.

THE HIGH COST OF MACHINERY AND SHIPPING, COMBINED WITH THE LOW PRICE OF GRAIN, DROVE THE FARMERS TO DESPERATION.

THIS WAS CLEARLY NO GOOD... HOW COULD BUSINESS SURVIVE IF NO ONE COULD AFFORD ANYTHING? SO, IN 1887, UNDER THE PRODDING OF PRESIDENT **GROVER CLEVELAND** CONGRESS TOOK THE FIRST STEP TOWARD GOVERNMENT REGULATION OF MONOPOLY.

(FIRST DEMOCRATIC PRESIDENT SINCE THE CIVIL WAR)

THEY CREATED THE INTERSTATE COMMERCE COMMISSION TO CONTROL THE RAILROADS' ERRATIC RATE SCHEDULES. BIG BUSINESS RECOILED IN HORROR!

BUT A FAR SIGHTED RAILROAD LAWYER POINTED OUT, "THE COMMISSION... CAN BE MADE OF GREAT USE TO THE RAILROAD... IT SATISFIES THE POPULAR CLAMOR FOR GOVERNMENT SUPERVISION...AT THE SAME TIME THAT THAT SUPERVISION IS ALMOST ENTIRELY NOMINAL. THE PART OF WISDOM IS NOT TO DESTROY THE COMMISSION BUT TO UTILIZE IT." THE WATCHDOG HAD NO TEETH!

COME, FIDO!

AS CONGRESS WENT ON TO PASS THE SIMILARLY TOOTHLESS **SHERMAN ANTI-TRUST ACT** IN 1890, FARMERS ROSE UP IN WHAT HAS BECOME KNOWN AS THE

POPULIST REVOLT.

RAISE LESS CORN AND MORE HELL!

—MARY LEASE

THEY FORMED THE ANTI-BANK, ANTI-BUSINESS *PEOPLE'S PARTY*, DEMANDING

☆ GOVERNMENT OWNER-SHIP OR REGULATION OF ALL MONOPOLIES

☆ EASY MONEY FOR DEBTORS

☆ AN INCOME TAX

IN THE 1892 PRESIDENTIAL ELECTION, THE POPULIST CANDIDATE CARRIED SIX STATES, AND WALL STREET FELT A NERVOUS TREMOR...

RUMBLE

63

THE '90'S ALSO MARKED
THE END OF THE FRONTIER.
THREE CENTURIES OF
INDIAN WARFARE HAD
FINALLY ENDED, AS
DIE-HARDS LIKE THE APACHE
GERONIMO SURRENDERED
TO RESERVATION LIFE.

IN 1889, THE GOVERNMENT EVEN OPENED "INDIAN TERRITORY"—OKLAHOMA—
TO WHITES. 50000 WAITED AT THE BORDER... AT A SIGNAL, THEY
MADE A MAD DASH TO SETTLE *SOONER* THAN THEIR NEIGHBORS,
AND A GREAT MUSICAL WAS BORN!!

OOO-OK-LAHOMA!!

A BRIEF FLARE-UP OF
INDIAN PRIDE, THE RELIGIOUS
GHOST DANCE MOVEMENT,
AROUSED THE WHITES' IRE.
SITTING BULL HIMSELF
WAS ASSASSINATED AS A
SUSPECTED SYMPATHIZER, AND
IN THE HYSTERIA, THE
ARMY GUNNED DOWN 300
UNARMED MEN, WOMEN,
AND CHILDREN AT SNOWY
WOUNDED KNEE, S.D.

AND
NOW THEY
CALL THEM
"GOOD"
INDIANS...

THE WEST WAS DIVIDED UP INTO TERRITORIES, WHICH WERE SETTLED BY PROUD, LEATHERY PEOPLE OF FEW WORDS AND POPULIST LEANINGS.

POSSIBLY THE WEST'S WILDEST INNOVATION WAS IN GIVING THE VOTE TO WOMEN (BEGINNING IN WYOMING IN 1870).

SO THIS WAS CAPITAL'S
DILEMMA IN THE 1890's:

THE ILL-PAID WORKER
CAN'T AFFORD OUR
PRODUCTS...

THE DEBT-RIDDEN
FARMER CAN'T AFFORD
OUR PRODUCTS...

THE EVER-EXPANDING
WEST HAS STOPPED
EXPANDING...

OR **HAS** IT?

FOR MANY YEARS,
AS EVERYONE KNEW,
THE EUROPEAN ANSWER
TO THESE PROBLEMS WAS

COLONIALISM.

OVERSEAS COLONIES
PROVIDED A POOL OF
LOW-PAID LABOR,
A SOURCE OF CHEAP
RAW MATERIALS, AND
A MARKET FOR
SURPLUS MANUFACTURED
GOODS!

WORKS LIKE
MAGIC!

SO—PERHAPS AMERICA
COULD KEEP EXPANDING—
INTO THE **PACIFIC!!**

WESTWARD
HO!

THE LIKELIEST THING IN THE PACIFIC WAS THE **PHILIPPINE ISLANDS**, A COLONY OF SPAIN.

SPAIN ALSO CONTROLLED CUBA AND PUERTO RICO, RIGHT IN THE U.S.A.'s BACK YARD...

HOW CONVENIENT!

SO... IN 1898, THE U.S. LAUNCHED THE **SPANISH-AMERICAN WAR.**

(OF COURSE, MANY AMERICANS, REMEMBERING HOW THEIR OWN NATION WAS BORN, WANTED NO COLONIES... SO THE COLONIALISTS DISGUISED THEIR AIMS UNDER A BANNER OF "LIBERATING THE FILIPINOS [CUBANS, PUERTO RICANS] FROM THE SPANISH YOKE.")

THIS IS ENLIGHTENING!

THANKS TO AMERICA'S MODERN NAVY, SPAIN WAS SUNK WITHIN FOUR MONTHS.

BUT SOME OF THE FILIPINOS MADE A FATAL MISTAKE: THEY TOOK THE RHETORIC SERIOUSLY. WHEN THE U.S. FAILED TO LEAVE THE ISLANDS, THEY ROSE UP IN AN INSURRECTION THAT ENDED ONLY AFTER THREE YEARS AND 600,000 FILIPINO DEAD.

IT HAS BEEN NECESSARY TO ADOPT WHAT WOULD IN OTHER COUNTRIES PROBABLY BE THOUGHT HARSH MEASURES,

SAID AN AMERICAN GENERAL.

AND SUDDENLY WE ENTER THE

20TH (CENTURY, THAT IS !!).

AN ANARCHIST'S BULLET FELLS PRESIDENT McKINLEY... THE VICE PRESIDENT, WAR HERO AND SPORTSMAN **THEODORE ROOSEVELT,** STEPS IN WITH A NEW AND MODERN APPROACH: *PROGRESSIVE REPUBLICANISM.*

ON THE ONE HAND, AN AGGRESSIVE FOREIGN POLICY: KEEP THE NEW COLONIES... TEAR OFF A PIECE OF COLOMBIA FOR A U.S.-CONTROLLED PANAMA CANAL... PUSH U.S. INTERESTS IN CHINA... SEND THE MARINES INTO CUBA AND THE DOMINICAN REPUBLIC...

MY FAVORITE WORD IS "BULLY"!

ON THE OTHER HAND, LIBERAL REFORMS AT HOME: MORE REGULATION OF BUSINESS... ENFORCEMENT OF THE ANTI-TRUST LAWS... CONSERVATION OF NATURAL RESOURCES AND WILDERNESS AREAS.*

* MOST EARLY CONSERVATIONISTS WERE SPORTSMEN WHO WANTED TO PRESERVE WILDLIFE IN ORDER TO HAVE AN OPPORTUNITY TO SHOOT IT.

BUT MANY LIBERALS DIDN'T
FEEL COMFORTABLE AMONG
THE REPUBLICANS.

AND VICE VERSA!

THE MORE ARDENT
AMONG THEM GRAVITATED
TOWARD TWO NEW
POLITICAL PARTIES, THE
SOCIALISTS
AND THE
PROGRESSIVES.

(THE POPULISTS HAD MEANWHILE
DISAPPEARED INTO THE DEMOCRATS.)

(THIS WAS ALSO THE ERA OF
MUCKRAKING JOURNALISM.)

EVEN AFTER ROOSEVELT
LEFT OFFICE IN 1908,
PROGRESSIVE PRESSURE
PRODUCED SUCH REFORMS
AS...

☆ THE INCOME
TAX (1913)

☆ DIRECT POPULAR
ELECTION OF
SENATORS (1913)

☆ FURTHER TRUST-
BUSTING, INCLUDING
THE BREAKUP
OF STANDARD OIL

IN **1912,** T.R. JUMPED
TO THE PROGRESSIVES,
RAN FOR PRESIDENT,
SPLIT THE REPUBLICAN VOTE...
AND A DEMOCRAT WAS
ELECTED — ONLY THE
SECOND SINCE BEFORE THE
CIVIL WAR —

⇒ WOODROW
WILSON.

(A
COLLEGE
PROFESSOR!)

IN THAT SAME ELECTION, THE SOCIALIST CANDIDATE

EUGENE DEBS

POLLED ALMOST A MILLION VOTES.

DESPITE PROGRESSIVE REFORMS, WORKERS' LIVES REMAINED HARD, WITH CHILD LABOR, SWEATSHOPS, PITIFUL WAGES, MASSACRES OF STRIKERS, AND GRISLY ACCIDENTS LIKE THE TRIANGLE SHIRTWAIST FACTORY FIRE, WHICH KILLED 146 WOMEN.

AHEM... I CAN SEE BOTH SIDES... I'M A PROFESSOR...

PRESIDENT WILSON RESPONDED LIBERALLY AT FIRST, CALLING FOR IMPROVEMENTS:

* WORKERS' COMPENSATION

* ANTI CHILD-LABOR LAWS

* LEGALIZATION OF ALL PEACEFUL PICKETING

BUT WILSON'S REFORMS WERE OFTEN STRUCK DOWN AS UNCONSTITUTIONAL BY CONSERVATIVE JUDGES.

WE NEED NOT REFORM BUT REVOLUTION!

ANARCHIST EMMA GOLDMAN

THANK THE LORD FOR CHECKS AND BALANCES!

BUT THESE SOCIALISTS WERE OPTIMISTS!

IT'S O.K.! CAPITALISM IS DOOMED!

SOON!

IN TIME FOR THE ELECTION!

ANY DAY NOW!

THE NATIONS OF EUROPE WERE AT EACH OTHERS' THROATS... THEIR CONTEST FOR COLONIES HAD COME TO A HEAD... TENSION MOUNTED..., ARMIES STOOD ON ALERT...

IN THE SUMMER OF '14, A SERB SHOT AN AUSTRIAN DUKE... IT FOLLOWED LOGICALLY THAT—

AUSTRIA HAD TO MENACE SERBIA...

RUSSIA HAD TO GROWL AT AUSTRIA...

GERMANY HAD TO ATTACK RUSSIA'S ALLY FRANCE...

ENGLAND HAD TO AID FRANCE...

AND, IN THIS RATIONAL FASHION, A

WORLD WAR BEGAN.

AS THE CARNAGE BEGAN, AMERICA WATCHED FROM THE SIDELINES. NOBODY WANTED TO GET INVOLVED!

YE GODS! WHO WOULD?!!

IT'S A BATTLE OF BRITISH CAPITAL AGAINST GERMAN CAPITAL, FOUGHT BY THE WORKERS!

THE SOCIALISTS WERE ESPECIALLY OUTSPOKEN AGAINST THE WAR.

THE DANGER, THEY SAW, WAS THAT AMERICAN BUSINESS WAS MUCH MORE CLOSELY TIED TO BRITAIN THAN TO GERMANY. ALREADY, U.S. MUNITIONS MAKERS WERE SHIPPING $ BILLIONS IN ARMS TO BRITAIN AND FRANCE — WITH U.S. BANKS DOING THE FINANCING...

... AND GERMAN SUBMARINES BEGAN SHOOTING TORPEDOES AT AMERICAN SHIPS.

PRESIDENT WILSON PREACHED NEUTRALITY WHILE PRACTICING PREPAREDNESS... IN THE **1916** PRESIDENTIAL CAMPAIGN, HIS SLOGAN WAS "HE KEPT US OUT OF WAR"!

BUT NO PROMISES!

BUT AMERICAN WEAPONS SHIPMENTS CONTINUED, AND SO DID THE SINKING OF AMERICAN SHIPS.

IN APRIL, 1917, ONE MONTH AFTER HIS SECOND INAUGURATION, WILSON CALLED FOR WAR AGAINST GERMANY... AND OFF MARCHED THE BOYS!

NO TO WAR

DON'T BUY THE BOSSES' WAR HYSTERIA! THINK FOR YOURSELF!

THAT WOULD BE ILLEGAL IN WARTIME.

... AND INTO THE JAILS WENT THE SOCIALISTS, FOR "OBSTRUCTING THE WAR EFFORT."

BUT TURMOIL CONTINUED, AS UNIONS LIKE THE

INDUSTRIAL **W**ORKERS OF THE **W**ORLD

KEPT UP THEIR STRIKES AND ANTI-WAR PROPAGANDA.

RESULT:

LYNCHINGS OF IWW, TRIALS OF IWW, AND, IN ONE CASE, HUNDREDS OF STRIKING COPPER MINERS AND THEIR FAMILIES LOCKED IN BOXCARS UNDER THE BROILING ARIZONA SUN.

AND THEN — A COMPLETE SURPRISE: THE COMMUNISTS CAME TO POWER IN

RUSSIA!!

·CHAPTER 5·

WAR AND PEACE AND WARREN HARDING

NEVER! NEVER WILL WE MAKE ALLIANCES WITH THE BRITISH AND AMERICAN CAPITALISTS, UNTIL 1940!

NEVER WILL WE ENGAGE IN IMPERIALISTIC WARFARE, EXCEPT IN COUNTRIES BEGINNING WITH THE LETTERS "H", "P", "L", "E", AND "AFGH!"

LENIN

NEVER! DO YOU HEAR ME? ALMOST NEVER!

THE RUSSIAN COMMUNISTS, OR **BOLSHEVIKS** (WHOSE FONDNESS FOR THE COLOR RED MIGHT JUSTIFY THE NAME BORSCH-EVIK), IMMEDIATELY PULLED OUT OF THE WAR, MAKING A SEPARATE PEACE WITH GERMANY.

WE HAD TO! OUR ARMY HAD STOPPED FIGHTING!

THIS MADE RUSSIA'S FORMER ALLIES HATE THEM EVEN MORE THAN THEY ALREADY HATED THEM FOR BEING COMMUNISTS.

WE'LL SETTLE THEIR HASH LATER!

THE ALLIES ACTUALLY INVADED RUSSIA... A DRIVE THAT OUTLASTED THE WORLD WAR, BUT FAILED (HAVE YOU NOTICED?) TO DISLODGE THE REDS.

MAKING PEACE WITH RUSSIA FREED GERMAN ARMIES TO TURN WESTWARD AGAINST FRANCE.

WUNDERBAR! NOW WE CAN LIE IN SOME *WARM* MUD!

THERE, IN MID-1918, THE AMERICANS HELPED HOLD THE LINE, THEN PUSH THE GERMANS BACK.

TAKE US TO YOUR LARDER!

BACK THROUGH THE RUINS THEY BATTLED... A FLU EPIDEMIC ADDED 800,000 DEATHS... AUSTRIA WITHDREW... AND FINALLY, THE GERMAN KAISER AGREED TO AN ARMISTICE ON NOV. 11, 1918.

When the fighting ended, everyone was exhausted, but Germany was more exhausted than anyone else.

So we were declared the losers!

President Wilson sailed to Europe with a plan called the **14 POINTS.** These pointed toward a peace based on justice, fairness, and self-determination.

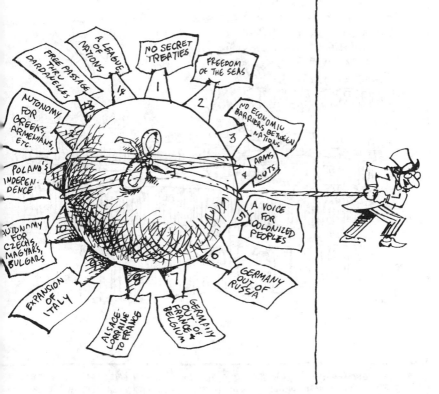

AT A SUMMIT MEETING IN VERSAILLES, FRANCE, THE PRIME MINISTERS OF BRITAIN AND FRANCE ENDORSED WOODROW WILSON'S CONCEPTS OF FAIRNESS, JUSTICE, AND SELF-DETERMINATION.

THEN THEY CONCOCTED A PEACE TREATY BASED ON RECRIMINATION, RETRIBUTION, AND REVENGE.* THIS WAS THE **TREATY OF VERSAILLES.**

* THE FRENCH LEADER, 79-YEAR-OLD GEORGES CLEMENCEAU, LEARNED THESE 3 R's IN HIS YOUTH WHILE SERVING IN THE U.S. JUST AFTER THE CIVIL WAR.

THE TREATY OF VERSAILLES...

...DICED & SLICED GERMANY AND AUSTRIA INTO A JULIENNE OF NEW NATIONS.

BEFORE

AFTER

...STRIPPED GERMANY OF HER OVERSEAS COLONIES AND HANDED THEM OVER TO BRITAIN AND FRANCE...

AND DID WE GIVE UP ANY OF OUR OWN? DON'T BE SILLY!

ANYTHING LEFT?

...SQUEEZED BILLIONS IN REPARATION PAYMENTS FROM AN ALREADY IMPOVERISHED GERMANY...

...AND CREATED THE FRAMEWORK FOR A LEAGUE OF NATIONS, AN INTERNATIONAL ORGANIZATION DESIGNED TO ENFORCE THE PEACE TREATY AND PREVENT FUTURE WAR.

O.K., WILSON, GO HOME AND SELL IT!

79

GLEEP!

WILSON RETURNED TO A NATION IN TYPICAL POST-WAR ECONOMIC TURMOIL: 100% INFLATION... STEELWORKERS, BRASS WORKERS, MINERS, THE ENTIRE CITY OF SEATTLE, EVEN MOVIE ACTORS ON STRIKE... STRIKERS SHOT... BOMBS EXPLODING... A SHIPLOAD OF RUSSIAN WEAPONS INTERCEPTED...

A FEW LEFTISTS ORGANIZED NOT ONE BUT TWO COMMUNIST PARTIES (INEVITABLY!).

THE REVOLUTION IS AT HAND!

YES, THE LEFT HAND!

THE RIGHT HAND!

LEFT!

RIGHT!

WE LEAVE NO SHEET UNTURNED!

ATTORNEY GENERAL **MITCHELL PALMER** (WHOSE OWN HOUSE WAS BOMBED) FORMED A SPECIAL INVESTIGATIVE UNIT UNDER 24-YEAR-OLD **J. EDGAR HOOVER.** HOOVER HAD REMARKABLE VISION — HE COULD SEE COMMUNISTS UNDER EVERY BED!!

IN JANUARY, 1920, BEGAN THE **PALMER RAIDS**. ARMED WITH HOOVER'S INTELLIGENCE, FEDERAL AGENTS ROUNDED UP THOUSANDS OF SUSPECTED ALIEN LEFTISTS, BEAT THEM UP, ARRAIGNED THEM WITHOUT DEFENSE ATTORNEYS, AND GENERALLY VIOLATED THEIR CONSTITUTIONAL RIGHTS.

FLOUT OUR TRADITIONS, WILL THEY??

BUT HOOVER'S "FACTS" WERE FAULTY. MOST OF THE "CRIMINALS" HAD TO BE FREED. THE REST, SOME 600, WERE DEPORTED TO RUSSIA.

THEN, AFTER A ROUGH CAMPAIGN THAT LEFT WILSON CRIPPLED FROM A STROKE, THE SENATE REJECTED THE PEACE TREATY, ON THE GROUNDS THAT A LEAGUE OF NATIONS WAS UNAMERICAN.

ENTANGLING ALLIANCES HAVE BEEN UNAMERICAN SINCE GEORGE WASHINGTON!

YET EVEN IN THE TEETH OF REACTION, THERE WERE PROGRESSIVE BRACES. IN 1919 AND '20's, CONGRESS MADE TWO FINAL ATTEMPTS TO PROGRESSIVIZE AMERICA:

WE'LL GET IT STRAIGHT YET!!

THE **18**TH AMENDMENT, BANNING THE SALE OF ALCOHOLIC DRINK...

SNIF

AND THE **19**TH,

WHICH GRANTED THE VOTE TO WOMEN.

AT LEAST WE WON'T LET 'EM INTO THE SALOONS — THERE WON'T BE ANY SALOONS!

SOB
SOB
SOB
SOB
SOB

IN A CURIOUS WAY, THESE REFORMS WERE LINKED.

HOW?

BOTH WENT BACK TO THE EARLY 1800's, WHEN PATRIARCHAL LAWS PLACED A WIFE'S PROPERTY ENTIRELY IN HER HUSBAND'S HANDS...

AT LEAST HE HAS HANDS!

AN ALCOHOLIC MAN COULD DRINK AWAY HIS WIFE'S WAGES, BELONGINGS, INHERITANCE, BECAUSE HE OWNED THEM!

AH! WHAT A SENSE OF SECURITY!

SO SALOON-BUSTERS AND FEMINISTS FORMED A TWO-PRONGED ATTACK ON THE PROBLEM: IMPROVE WOMEN'S LEGAL STATUS, AND REDUCE ALCOHOLISM!

IF I HAVE MY PROPERTY, I CAN LEAVE THE LUSH!

LATER, PROGRESSIVES JOINED THE TEMPERANCE FORCES TO PROMOTE CIVIC EFFICIENCY, IMPROVE PUBLIC MORALS, AND PROTECT THE NATION'S STRATEGIC GRAIN SUPPLY, SO THE DOUGHBOYS WOULD HAVE BREAD IN THE WAR.

A SOBER ARMY KILLS **MUCH** MORE EFFICIENTLY!

SMESH!

THE RESULT WAS THE 18TH AMENDMENT.

MEANWHILE, WOMEN'S RIGHTS GROUPS NEVER QUIT PETITIONING, LOBBYING, MARCHING, AND DEMONSTRATING — FOR EXAMPLE, AT THE **STATUE OF LIBERTY** DEDICATION IN 1886.

CAN YOU VOTE, BABE?

THE STRUGGLE HEATED UP IN THE 19-TEENS. AT WILSON'S 1913 INAUGURAL, A SUFFRAGE MARCH TURNED INTO A RIOT!

MOST UNSEEMLY!

IN MOST WESTERN STATES, WOMEN WERE ALREADY VOTING WITHOUT DISASTER ... SO IN LATE 1920, CONGRESS FINALLY GAVE IN.

84

AND SO CAME NOVEMBER, **1920**, AND THE FIRST ELECTION IN WHICH WOMEN VOTED NATIONWIDE.

IT'S THE END! LOOK AT THAT HEMLINE!

ANTI-FEMINISTS HAD ALWAYS SCREAMED THAT WOMEN WITH RIGHTS WOULD "TURN INTO MEN"... AND IT TURNED OUT THEY WERE RIGHT, IN ONE RESPECT, ANYWAY: WOMEN **VOTED** EXACTLY LIKE MEN!

HAD TO! THERE WERE NO WOMEN CANDIDATES!

DEBS, THE SOCIALIST, DREW 900,000 VOTES. COX, THE DEMOCRAT, MANAGED 10 TIMES THAT MANY...

IS THAT GOOD?

... WHILE THE REPUBLICAN, **WARREN HARDING**, WITH THE SLOGAN "BACK TO NORMALCY," PILED UP **16 MILLION**, AN 8-TO-5 LANDSLIDE!! AND WHAT WAS NORMALCY???

FORGETTABLE REPUBLICAN PRESIDENTS, CORRUPTION, LIGHT TAXES ON THE RICH, A BOOM, AND A CRASH!

TO SYMBOLIZE NORMALCY, THE NEW ADMINISTRATION MADE A BONFIRE OF HUNDREDS OF USED WARPLANES.

THEN HARDING'S MEN CRUSHED A STEEL STRIKE, BUSTED SOME UNIONS, EASED ANTI-TRUST ENFORCEMENT, TOOK A FEW BRIBES, AND SLIPPED THE NAVY'S STRATEGIC OIL RESERVES INTO PRIVATE HANDS. THEIR PHILOSOPHY WAS EXPRESSED IN FIVE WORDS OF TREASURY SECRETARY ANDREW MELLON (A MILLIONAIRE): "LIGHT TAXES ON THE RICH."

BUT THIS WAS NORMALCY WITH A DIFFERENCE:

ALTHOUGH REPUBLICANS HAD ALWAYS WELCOMED IMMIGRANTS AS FACTORY-FODDER, NOW THEY DECIDED THAT FOREIGNERS CAUSED INDUSTRIAL INDIGESTION. THE ADMINISTRATION CUT IMMIGRATION FROM 600,000 TO 60,000 A YEAR.

* * * * * * * * * * * * QUOTAS FAVORED NORTHERN EUROPEANS. THE ANNUAL LIMIT FOR JAPAN DROPPED FROM 185 TO **ZERO.**

WE'LL GIVE YOU A "ZERO!"

RACISM SURGED AS NEVER BEFORE... IT WAS WORLDWIDE... WHILE HITLER SURFACED IN GERMANY, THE **Ku Klux Klan** HAD AMAZING SUCCESS IN THE U.S.A. THE KKK WAS NO LONGER ONLY ANTI-BLACK —

WE'RE ANTI-RED!

ANTI-JEW!

ANTI-CATHOLIC!

ANTI-IMMIGRANT!

WE DON'T THINK MUCH OF EACH OTHER!

AT ITS PEAK, THE KLAN CLAIMED SOME **5 MILLION** MEMBERS!

THE FLIP SIDE OF RACISM IS ETHNIC NATIONALISM... AND, LIKE THE SERBS, BULGARS, ZIONISTS, AND OTHERS CRAVING NATIONHOOD, BLACK AMERICANS NOW RESPONDED *EN MASSE* TO A BACK-TO-AFRICA MOVEMENT LED BY

MARCUS "MESSIAH" **GARVEY.**

GARVEY'S BLEND OF MUSSOLINI-STYLE UNIFORMS AND DISCIPLINE WITH BLACK PRIDE, BLACK ENTERPRISE, AND RACIAL PURITY WON MANY FOLLOWERS, ESPECIALLY AMONG THE POOR...

TO OUR KOMMON GOAL:

NO MORE KREAM IN THE KOFFEE!

...AS WELL AS THE FRIENDSHIP OF THE KU KLUX KLAN, WITH WHOM GARVEY HELD SEVERAL KOZY KOFFEE KLATCHES !!

WE WERE THE ORIGINAL FASCISTS,

HE SAID LATER...

88

ANOTHER TWIST ON NORMALCY WAS

PROHIBITION

"OF THE STUFF THAT LOWERS INHIBITIONS

THE LAW INTENDED TO RAISE PUBLIC MORALS SIMULTANEOUSLY LOWERED THEM. WITH LIQUOR OUTLAWED, ONLY OUTLAWS DISTRIBUTED LIQUOR... GANGSTERS THRIVED...

BLADDA BLADDA

...AND OF COURSE SO DID THE G-MEN!!

OUR MISSION: TO PROTECT THE PUBLIC FROM BEVERAGES, FOREIGN AND DOMESTIC!

THIS SIDE UP→

A GHASTLY SIGHT!

I CAN BARELY STOP LOOKING AT IT...

COURT ORDER

ANOTHER SURPRISING EFFECT OF PROHIBITION:

IN 1917, THE "DRYS" CLOSED THE DANCE HALLS, SALOONS, AND BROTHELS OF NEW ORLEANS' FABLED STORYVILLE SECTION.

OUT-OF-WORK STORYVILLE MUSICIANS LIKE **JELLY ROLL MORTON, KING OLIVER, KID ORY, AND LOUIS ARMSTRONG** JOINED A GENERAL BLACK MIGRATION NORTH TO ST. LOUIS, K.C., CHICAGO, AND HARLEM.

ORY   ARMSTRONG   MORTON   OLIVER

BY THE 1920's, THEIR MUSIC HAD A NEW NAME:

JAZZ!

"AN UNLOOSING OF INSTINCTS THAT NATURE WISELY HAS TAUGHT US TO HOLD WELL IN CHECK." *

*ATLANTIC MONTHLY, 1922

WHITE MUSICIANS JUMPED ON THE JAZZ-WAGON. WHITES FLOCKED TO BLACK CLUBS FOR ILLICIT THRILLS... SEX WAS IN... HEMLINES ROSE... HOLLYWOOD GLAMORIZED THE ACTION... THE FIRST TALKING FILM WAS "THE JAZZ SINGER" IN 1927... AND JAZZ BECAME THE FIRST AUTHENTIC ART FORM MADE IN AMERICA!

JUNK THAT JIVE! JAZZ IS **HOT!**

CHARLESTON, CHARLESTON...

THEY CALLED IT THE JAZZ AGE, THE ROARING 20's, THE WHOOPEE ERA, THE LAWLESS DECADE— BUT IN FACT, IT WAS REALLY PRETTY DRY... MORE AMERICANS THAN EVER WORKED HARD AND STAYED STONE-COLD SOBER!!

SIGH

IN
OUT

As people worked hard, business boomed...

The stock market sizzled like a Louis Armstrong solo...

...Until one horrible Wall Street week, culminating on "Black Tuesday", Oct. 29, '29.

Stock prices plunged, and so did a number of bankers and brokers!

CHAPTER 6

SHOCK THERAPY FOR A GREAT DEPRESSION

"HITLER, HAVING ENDED
UNEMPLOYMENT IN GERMANY,
HAD GONE ON TO END IT
FOR HIS ENEMIES."
—JOHN KENNETH GALBRAITH

THE CAUSES OF THIS
GREAT CRASH WERE OBSCURE,
ESPECIALLY WHEN
COMPARED TO ITS
EFFECTS, WHICH
WERE SPLATTERED
ALL OVER THE
SIDEWALK.

ONE THEORY IS THAT THE BOOM ITSELF WAS TO BLAME FOR THE CRASH: FACTORIES CHURNED OUT GOODS FASTER THAN PEOPLE COULD BUY THEM!

BUY! EAT! CONSUME!

THIS IS CALLED A CRISIS OF

OVER-SUPPLY.

BUT, IF ONE PART OF A HISTORIAN'S JOB IS TO UNCOVER THE CAUSES OF THINGS, THERE'S ANOTHER PART, TOO — DISAGREEING WITH OTHER HISTORIANS!

FOR ANOTHER INTERPRETATION, SEE THE NEXT PAGE!

NO, DON'T!

CALLING IT

OVERSUPPLY, AFTER ALL, IGNORES THE HUMAN ELEMENT—JUST WHO WAS SUPPOSED TO BUY, BUY, BUY?

MILLIONS OF FARMERS

AND UNSKILLED WORKERS, UNTOUCHED BY THE BOOM, EKED OUT A LIVING ON THE EDGE OF BANKRUPTCY.

PLAYIN' BLUES, NOT JAZZ!

ANTI-UNION POLICIES

ENSURED THAT WAGES COULDN'T GROW AS FAST AS PRICES OR PROFITS...

...SO **UNDER-DEMAND** MIGHT BE A BETTER NAME FOR THE PROBLEM.

AH, FOR A CONSUMER WHO ISN'T A FARMER OR WORKER!

CONSEQUENTLY,

INVESTORS FUNNELLED PROFITS INTO SPECULATION RATHER THAN EXPANDING PRODUCTION.

PYRAMID SCHEMES, MERGERS, ETC...

STOCK PRICES

SPIRALLED UPWARD. PROFITS SWELLED—ON PAPER—

UNTIL, ONE DAY, TOO

MANY INVESTORS CASHED IN. THE MARKET DIPPED...PEOPLE BEGAN SELLING IN SELF-DEFENSE...AND THEN IN PANIC. IN SHORT, THE MARKET CRASHED.

FREE MARKET

ECONOMIES TEND TO REPEAT THIS PATTERN, MANY HISTORIANS AGREE.

OH... SWELL...

And now we pass from causes to effects...

With paper profits gone, people were forced to use real money. It turned out to be pretty scarce...

Prices plummeted...

So did wages...

Businesses folded or shrank...

Half the nation's banks failed, drained by panicky depositors...

Millions lost their jobs, houses, farms...

Breadlines swelled... (Privately run, of course — the government gave no handouts!!)

A TRIUMPH OF VOLUNTARIS[M]

THE PRESIDENT, **HERBERT HOOVER,** BELIEVED THAT PUBLIC CONFIDENCE WAS THE KEY TO RECOVERY... SO HE KEPT SAYING, "PROSPERITY IS JUST AROUND THE CORNER."

BUT IT WASN'T... IN FACT, THINGS ONLY GOT WORSE...

THIS ONE MAKES MY OTHER DEPRESSIONS LOOK LIKE LITTLE MOOD SWINGS...

PROSPERITY IS —OW!

THE ELECTORATE DID THE ONLY CONCEIVABLE THING, AND OUT WENT HOOVER IN 1932.

IN HIS PLACE THEY ELECTED THE DEMOCRAT

FRANKLIN D. ROOSEVELT,

A GOLDEN-TONGUED COUSIN OF TEDDY'S, WHO USED THE NEW-FANGLED MEDIUM OF THE RADIO NETWORK TO SPEAK DIRECTLY TO ALL.

WE HAVE NOTHING TO FEAR BUT FEAR ITSELF! — HE SAID. —

THIS STATEMENT, LIKE MANY ANOTHER FAMOUS PHRASE, IS NOT ESPECIALLY EASY TO UNDERSTAND.

WOW!

WHAT?

WHAT IT MEANT WAS THAT ROOSEVELT WASN'T AFRAID TO TRY **ANYTHING!**

FOR INSTANCE...

NRA: BUSINESS SLUMPING? WAGES FALLING? LAYOFFS RISING? THE **N**ATIONAL **R**ECOVERY **A**CT SET WAGE, PRICE, AND EMPLOYMENT GUIDELINES (LATER DECLARED UNCONSTITUTIONAL).

AAA: FARM PRICES FALLING? THE **A**GRICULTURAL **A**DJUSTMENT **A**CT PAID FARMERS TO DESTROY PRODUCE!

NOW WAIT A MINUTE!

SSI: OLD PEOPLE DESTITUTE? **S**OCIAL **S**ECURITY **I**NSURANCE GIVES A PENSION TO EVERY RETIRED PERSON.

GERMANY HAS HAD IT SINCE THE 1870'S!

WPA: ARTISTS UNEMPLOYED? THE **W**ORKS **P**ROGRESS **A**DMINISTRATION HIRED THEM.

SUDDENLY I LOVE THE GOVERNMENT AND MUST EXPLAIN WHY IN A SERIES OF ENORMOUS MURALS...

PWA POURED MONEY INTO PUBLIC **WORKS** —DAMS, BRIDGES, HIGHWAYS.

FDIC SAVED BANKS BY INSURING DEPOSITS.

TVA CREATED A FEDERALLY OWNED UTILITY WHICH ELECTRIFIED THE TENNESSEE VALLEY.

AND PROHIBITION IS REPEALED!

THIS IMPROVISED STRUCTURE OF WELFARE, JOB PROGRAMS, AND ECONOMIC PLANNING WAS CALLED THE

NEW DEAL

OUR MOTTO: WHATEVER WORKS!

THE NEW DEAL TRANSFORMED AMERICA WITH A NEW SENSE OF THE GOVERNMENT'S ROLE.

IT MADE ROOSEVELT THE MOST POPULAR PRESIDENT IN OUR HISTORY — AND ONE OF THE MOST HATED. CONSERVATIVES, UNABLE TO UTTER HIS NAME WITHOUT GAGGING, DENOUNCED "THAT MAN" AS A TRAITOR TO HIS CLASS!

> TWO NAMES YOU DON'T SAY OUT LOUD: GOD'S AND **THAT MAN'S!!**

THIS WAS ODD, BECAUSE ROOSEVELT'S PROGRAM WAS INTENDED TO STRENGTHEN CAPITALISM — TO SAVE IT FROM ITSELF, YOU MIGHT SAY. ROOSEVELT CONFISCATED NOTHING, NATIONALIZED NO INDUSTRY,* AND NOBODY SAW BUSINESSMEN GOING BROKE AS A RESULT OF THE NEW DEAL!!

> THAT'S HOW SNEAKY HE IS!

*ALTHOUGH, WHEN THE MEXICAN GOVERNMENT NATIONALIZED AMERICAN OIL COMPANIES, ROOSEVELT REFUSED TO DEFEND THE COMPANIES' INFLATED CLAIMS.

100

SO... WHAT WAS TO HATE?? WELL... **WELFARE** AND GOVERNMENT ASSISTANCE, WHICH SUPPOSEDLY SAP PEOPLE'S INITIATIVE AND SELF-RELIANCE.

DEFICIT SPENDING, I.E., FINANCING GOVERNMENT PROGRAMS THROUGH BORROWING RATHER THAN TAXES. IT STIMULATED THE ECONOMY, BUT SOUNDED UNSOUND, BUSINESSWISE!

(LATER, CONSERVATIVES DID IT, TOO...)

ROOSEVELT RECOGNIZED THE **SOVIET UNION,** AND CEASED PERSECUTING COMMUNISTS AT HOME — AND PARTY MEMBERSHIP AND INFLUENCE SWELLED.

AND FINALLY, THERE WAS HIS LENIENT ATTITUDE TOWARD **ORGANIZED LABOR.**

LABOR IN THE '30's

AS THE NEW DEAL BEGAN, THE ONLY LABOR ORGANIZATION TO SPEAK OF WAS

THE **AFL.** (SEE P. 53.)

AFL UNIONS WERE **CRAFT** UNIONS— MEANING THAT EACH UNION REPRESENTED ONE SKILL:

MACHINISTS
ELECTRICIANS
WELDERS
PLUMBERS
CARPENTERS
PAINTERS
:

BUT

THE AFL IGNORED THE LOWEST-PAID, UNSKILLED, AND SEMI-SKILLED WORKERS.

IT RESISTED RACIAL INTEGRATION, VIEWING BLACKS AS LOW-WAGE COMPE-TITION.

AND KEEPING US THAT WAY!

DITTO FOR WOMEN, HISPANICS, CHINESE...

THE CHINESE MUST GO! *

* CONSTANT REFRAIN OF 1880's SAN FRANCISCO LABOR LEADER DENNIS KEARNY.

IT'S A GAIN FOR SOME ON THE BACKS OF OTHERS!

EVER SINCE DEBS, THE LEFT WING OF THE LABOR MOVEMENT HAD BLASTED THE AFL'S POLICY OF DIVIDING THE WORKING CLASS.

THE LEFTISTS FAVORED UNIONS ORGANIZED ON

INDUSTRIAL

LINES: EACH UNION REPRESENTING AN ENTIRE INDUSTRY:

MINEWORKERS
LONGSHOREMEN
STEELWORKERS
AUTO WORKERS
ETC.

THE WAY TO END LOW-WAGE COMPETITION BY BLACKS, IN THIS VIEW, WAS TO BRING THEM INTO THE UNIONS!!

103

AS THE DEPRESSION DRAGGED ON, INDUSTRIAL WORKERS BEGAN DEMANDING UNION PROTECTION.. TACTICS TURNED MILITANT, WITH MASS PICKETING, 1000 AT A TIME, AND "FLYING PICKETS" ATTACKING STRIKEBREAKERS.

IN **1934** CAME THE FIRST BIG SUCCESSES: A VICTORIOUS TEAMSTER STRIKE IN MINNEAPOLIS...

A WEST COAST LONGSHORE STRIKE, WHICH BECAME A GENERAL STRIKE IN SAN FRANCISCO.

BUT THE AFL WAS PARALYZED BY JURISDICTIONAL DISPUTES. ITS CRAFT UNIONS WANTED TO DIVIDE UP THE FACTORY WORKERS— A GUARANTEED WAY TO UNIONIZE **SOME** OF THEM... BUT THE WORKERS WOULD HAVE NONE OF IT, SO IN 1935 EIGHT OF THE "PROGRESSIVE" UNIONS FORMED THE **C**OMMITTEE FOR **I**NDUSTRIAL **O**RGANIZATION, HEADED BY MINEWORKERS PRESIDENT **JOHN L. LEWIS.**

PUNCHING "BIG BILL" HUTCHESON IN THE NOSE AT AFL CONVENTION

THE CIO, WHICH
HAD MANY COMMUNIST
ORGANIZERS,
ENDORSED AN EVEN
MORE MILITANT
TACTIC: THE
SIT-DOWN,
OR PLANT SEIZURE.

SURPRISE!!

THE MOST FAMOUS SIT-
DOWN STRIKE WAS AGAINST
GENERAL MOTORS, IN
DECEMBER - JANUARY, 1936.

WITH THE TEMPERATURE DOWN
TO 16°, MANAGEMENT SHUT
OFF THE HEAT AND
STOPPED THE FOOD.
WORKERS BLASTED THE
POLICE WITH ICY WATER
AND PELTED THEM WITH
SMALL CAR PARTS — THE
"BATTLE OF BULLS RUN." *

AT OTHER PLANTS,
WORKERS FLOCKED
TO THE UNION... THE
STRIKE SPREAD... AND
AT LAST GENERAL MOTORS
WAS FORCED TO
SIT DOWN WITH THE
UNITED
AUTO
WORKERS.

IT'S ALL
THAT MAN'S
FAULT!!

* "BULLS" = POLICE.

NOW WE ASK: HOW WELL DID THE NEW DEAL WORK??

AND WE ANSWER: GOVERNMENT SPENDING DID STIMULATE THE ECONOMY, CREATE JOBS, BUILD BRIDGES, DAMS, AND ART DECO POST OFFICES.

WELFARE PROGRAMS RELIEVED SOME ANXIETY... GOVERNMENT INSURANCE ENDED BANK PANICS... UNIONIZATION IMPROVED WAGES AND WORKING CONDITIONS FOR THE EMPLOYED.

RESULT: ROOSEVELT WON RE-ELECTION IN '36 BY A LANDSLIDE.

YEAH!

BUT — RECOVERY WAS SLOW... INDUSTRY REMAINED SLACK... AND, WHEN "PRUDENT" SPENDING TRIMS WERE MADE, THE ECONOMY TOOK A DIVE THAT SENT UNEMPLOYMENT ALMOST TO 1933 LEVELS!!

NOW WHAT?

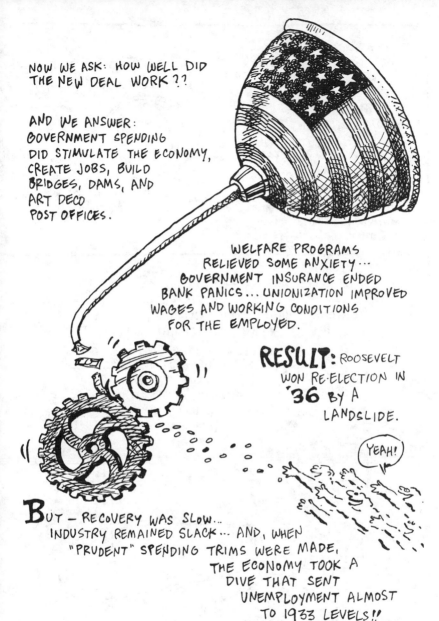

THE ANSWER CAME FROM ABROAD, WHERE LINGERING HATREDS FROM WORLD WAR I WERE EXPLODING...
IN '31, JAPAN INVADED MANCHURIA... IN '35 ITALY INVADED ETHIOPIA... THE DEMOCRACIES STOOD BY AND DEPLORED THESE MOVES, WHICH WERE, AFTER ALL, IN A TIME-HONORED TRADITION OF COLONIAL CONQUEST.

WE DEPLORE NOT DOING IT FIRST, THAT IS—

AND THEN THERE WAS GERMANY... IN '33, JUST BEFORE ROOSEVELT'S INAUGURAL, THE NAZI **ADOLF HITLER** CAME TO POWER... THIS NAZISM WAS A SORT OF GERMAN-POTENTIAL MOVEMENT...

HITLER WANTED GERMANS TO FEEL GOOD ABOUT THEMSELVES— BY THINKING ILL OF EVERYBODY ELSE, ESPECIALLY JEWS.

I'M O.K., YOU'RE DEAD!

AT FIRST, HITLER'S ECONOMIC PROGRAM WAS AMAZINGLY LIKE ROOSEVELT'S: DEFICIT SPENDING AND PUBLIC WORKS... BUT HITLER HAD CERTAIN ADVANTAGES: A DEMONIC WORLD VIEW, ABSOLUTE POWER, NO PRUDENCE —SO HE CURED UNEMPLOYMENT MORE EFFECTIVELY THAN FDR!

IT ISN'T FAIR!

BUT THAT WASN'T ENOUGH... HITLER'S DEMENTED IDEAS OF NORDIC SUPERIORITY CALLED FOR A BIGGER GERMANY, MORE GERMANS, AND FEWER "INFERIORS."

GOD! SOUNDS ALL TOO FAMILIAR!

SO, WHEN HE SWALLOWED AUSTRIA AND CZECHOSLOVAKIA, IT WAS OBVIOUS THAT WAR WAS COMING, AND THE DEMOCRACIES TREMBLED AT THE PROSPECT—

FULL EMPLOYMENT AT LAST?!!

109

1939: HITLER STUNS THE WORLD BY MAKING FRIENDS WITH HIS ARCH-ENEMY STALIN*...THEN INVADES POLAND.

BY MID-**1940** THE GERMANS HAVE OCCUPIED SCANDINAVIA, BELGIUM, HOLLAND, AND FRANCE, AND BUSILY BOMB BRITAIN...

WE'LL SAVE YOU, WINSTON!

THE U.S. IS OFFICIALLY NEUTRAL, BUT HITLER IS OBVIOUSLY DANGEROUS... SO WAR PREPARATIONS BEGIN... ARMS FACTORIES CRANK UP...WEAPONS SALES RESUME (CASH & CARRY ONLY!)... ROOSEVELT — WITHOUT CONGRESSIONAL APPROVAL — SHIPS 50 DESTROYERS TO BRITAIN AND OBTAINS 8 MILITARY BASES IN RETURN...

...AND THERE'S A PRESIDENTIAL ELECTION... ROOSEVELT RUNS AGAIN AND WINS AGAIN, THE FIRST 3-TERM PRESIDENT...

* DICTATOR OF THE USSR

1941: JAPAN MOVES INTO FRENCH INDOCHINA (VIETNAM), THREATENING DUTCH, BRITISH, AND AMERICAN COLONIAL AND COMMERCIAL INTERESTS IN THE INDIES, BURMA, THE PHILIPPINES...

HITLER DOUBLE-CROSSES STALIN AND INVADES RUSSIA — A VAST BLUNDER, BUT IT CEMENTS AN ALLIANCE WITH JAPAN...

THE U.S. CUTS OFF OIL SHIPMENTS TO JAPAN... CONGRESS BEGINS LENDING WEAPONS TO HITLER'S FOES... JAPAN AND THE U.S. TRADE IMPOSSIBLE DEMANDS...

AND THEN...

ON DEC. 7, JAPAN BOMBED THE AMERICAN NAVY BASE AT PEARL HARBOR, HAWAII, WIPING OUT BATTLESHIPS, PLANES, AND MORE THAN 1500 LIVES.

CONGRESS NATURALLY DECLARED WAR ON JAPAN, AND WITHIN DAYS GERMANY AND ITALY HAD JOINED IN.– MERRY CHRISTMAS!

SUPERB SMELL!

WITH MOBILIZATION, THE ECONOMY BOOMED... FACTORIES RETOOLED FOR WAR... UNEMPLOYMENT VANISHED... INFLATION WAS CHECKED BY GOVERNMENT PRICE CONTROLS... UNIONS PLEDGED NOT TO STRIKE – AND NO ONE WORRIED ABOUT POLLUTION...

MASSIVE POPULATION SHIFTS TOOK PLACE... A STREAM
OF SOUTHERN BLACKS FLOWED NORTH, TOWARD
THE FACTORY JOBS OF DETROIT,
SAN FRANCISCO, CHICAGO...

TRADITIONAL DISCRIMINATION
GAVE WAY A LITTLE...
WOMEN DID HEAVY
FACTORY WORK...

MY MOM AT
THE SHIPYARDS

AND YET — OVER 100,000 JAPANESE-AMERICANS (80% OF THEM
CITIZENS) WERE ROUNDED UP AS "SECURITY RISKS" AND
INTERNED IN CAMPS FOR THE DURATION.

(AN IRONY OF THE WAR WAS
THAT AMERICAN PROPAGANDA
DEPICTED THE JAPANESE AS
INHUMAN — WHILE HITLER, WHO
REALLY WAS A MONSTER,
USUALLY APPEARED AS A
COMIC-OPERA BUFFOON.)

THAT HITLER
WAS PRETTY
SMART TO BE
BORN WHITE!

113

IN EUROPE, THE UNITED STATES AVOIDED A DIRECT GROUND ASSAULT AGAINST GERMANY, UNTIL THE GERMANS WERE WORN OUT BY RUSSIA... MEANWHILE, ALLIED BOMBERS BLASTED GERMAN INDUSTRY, WHICH OF COURSE WAS OFTEN LOCATED IN GERMAN CITIES. IN HAMBURG THE FIRESTORM KILLED 50,000 CIVILIANS; IN DRESDEN, 100,000 PLUS...

...WHILE ARMORED DIVISIONS INVADED NORTH AFRICA, FROM WHICH POINT THEY PUSHED INTO ITALY.

AT LAST, IN JUNE OF '44, UNDER GENERAL **DWIGHT D. EISENHOWER**, THE ALLIES INVADED FRANCE... AND EIGHT MONTHS LATER, MET THE RUSSIANS IN BERLIN.

ROOSEVELT, CHURCHILL, AND STALIN MET TO DIVIDE UP THE POST-WAR WORLD — RATHER TO BRITAIN'S DISADVANTAGE...

WE'LL TAKE MILITARY BASES HERE, HERE, HERE, HERE, HERE, HERE...

WE'LL TAKE THIS.

114

THE PACIFIC WAR COMBINED
CARRIER-BASED NAVAL
ENGAGEMENTS WITH JUNGLE
WARFARE IN THE PHILIPPINES,
OKINAWA, ETC... THE SEA
BATTLES WERE THE FIRST
IN HISTORY IN WHICH THE
ENEMIES' FLEETS REMAINED
COMPLETELY OUT OF EYESHOT!

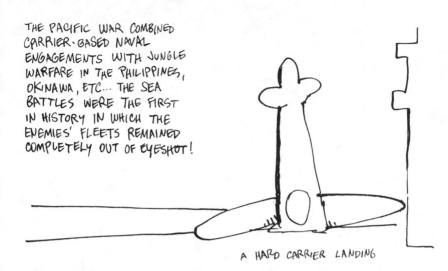

A HARD CARRIER LANDING

BY MID-1945, JAPAN WAS ENCIRCLED... FROM ISLAND BASES
AMERICAN HEAVY BOMBERS LEVELLED TOKYO...

THE AMERICANS, PERHAPS TOO FULL OF THEIR
SMASHING VICTORY OVER HITLER, DEMANDED
NOTHING LESS THAN UNCONDITIONAL SURRENDER...
THE JAPANESE SENSE OF HONOR WOULD NOT
ALLOW SUCH HUMILIATION... FURTHER NEGOTIATION
MIGHT HAVE PRODUCED A FACE-SAVING SOLUTION...
BUT TIME WAS SHORT: THE U.S.S.R. WAS
ABOUT TO DECLARE WAR ON JAPAN, AND
PRESIDENT TRUMAN* DIDN'T WANT TO
SHARE THE ISLANDS!!

SO...

*ROOSEVELT HAD DIED, WITH MUCH PUBLIC MOURNING, IN APRIL, '45.

CHAPTER 7

○ BRIGHT, WHITE LIGHT ○

AND TECHNOLOGY BEGAT INDUSTRY...
AND INDUSTRY BEGAT CAPITALISM...
AND CAPITALISM BEGAT COMMUNISM...
AND COMMUNISM BEGAT ANTI-COMMUNISM...
AND ANTI-COMMUNISM BEGAT FASCISM...

AH, TECHNOLOGY!

During the war years, the top-secret **MANHATTAN PROJECT** brought together America's top nuclear scientists to invent the first truly planet-threatening piece of technology.

It burst on Hiroshima on August 6, 1945... on Nagasaki, August 9...

So — years before anyone noticed acid rain, ozone depletion, or the greenhouse effect, people sensed a whiff of a breath of an inkling that something was dreadfully wrong...

This led to the familiar JITTERY feeling of the post-war world...

AND WHAT A WORLD... A GLOBE SHRUNKEN BY
COMMUNICATION AND TRANSPORTATION TECHNOLOGY... TWO
COUNTRIES, THE U.S. & U S S R, IMMENSELY SWOLLEN IN
POWER... ALMOST IMMEDIATELY, THE TWO ERSTWHILE
ALLIES BEGAN GROWLING LIKE A COUPLE OF MALE DOGS
IN A SMALL CLOSET.

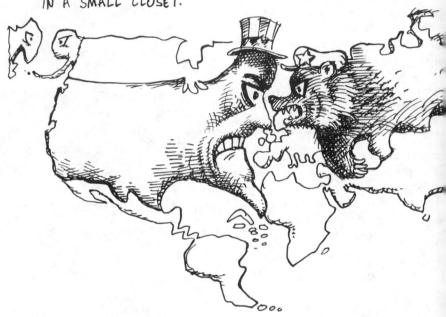

IT'S REALLY AMAZING
HOW FAST THEIR ALLIANCE
COLLAPSED. THE

UNITED
NATIONS,

ORGANIZED IN A
LOVE-FEAST MOOD
IN MID-'45,
DESCENDED INTO
DIPLOMATIC EAR-
BITING BY 1946.

GRRRR ARF
ARF YIP YIP YIP
BARK BARK

IT'S
GOOD TO
TALK.

THE U.S. DENOUNCED THE SOVIET OCCUPATION OF EASTERN EUROPE AND THE INSTALLATION OF COMMUNIST GOVERNMENTS THERE.

THE USSR COMPLAINED ABOUT THE EXPANDING U.S. ROLE IN THE WORLD, TO THE EXCLUSION OF THE SOVIET UNION.

IN GREECE, A CIVIL WAR PITTED RUSSIAN-BACKED GUERRILLAS AGAINST A U.S.-BACKED FASCIST KING.

FRANCE AND ITALY BOTH HAD LARGE COMMUNIST PARTIES.

GERMANY WAS DIVIDED INTO BRITISH, FRENCH, RUSSIAN, AND AMERICAN ZONES. BERLIN, THOUGH IN THE RUSSIAN ZONE, WAS JOINTLY HELD.

WHEN NEGOTIATIONS ON GERMANY FAILED, RUSSIA BLOCKADED BERLIN. THE U.S. AIRLIFTED SUPPLIES UNTIL THE USSR RELENTED.

WITH RELATIONS IN RUINS, PRESIDENT TRUMAN IN 1948 ANNOUNCED A NEW U.S. POLICY: THE GLOBAL

CONTAINMENT

OF COMMUNISM.

IF WE HAVE TO PEE ON EVERY TREE ON EARTH!

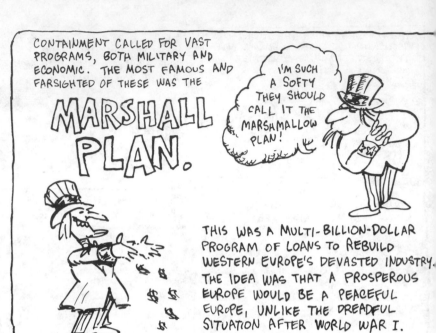

CONTAINMENT CALLED FOR VAST PROGRAMS, BOTH MILITARY AND ECONOMIC. THE MOST FAMOUS AND FARSIGHTED OF THESE WAS THE

MARSHALL PLAN.

I'M SUCH A SOFTY THEY SHOULD CALL IT THE MARSHMALLOW PLAN!

THIS WAS A MULTI-BILLION-DOLLAR PROGRAM OF LOANS TO REBUILD WESTERN EUROPE'S DEVASTED INDUSTRY. THE IDEA WAS THAT A PROSPEROUS EUROPE WOULD BE A PEACEFUL EUROPE, UNLIKE THE DREADFUL SITUATION AFTER WORLD WAR I.

THE MARSHALL PLAN WAS CALCULATED TO PAY CERTAIN DIVIDENDS: TO UNIFY WESTERN EUROPE AGAINST COMMUNISM; TO PENETRATE EUROPE'S ECONOMY WITH AMERICAN CAPITAL; AND TO CREATE A PROFITABLE CLIMATE FOR TRADE AND EXPANSION.

COME, LITTLE FISHIES!

THE POST-WAR PERIOD MARKED A
BASIC SHIFT IN U.S. FOREIGN POLICY:
EVER SINCE GEORGE WASHINGTON, THE
NATION HAD AVOIDED MILITARY ALLIANCES
WITH FOREIGN POWERS. NOW, THE
U.S. ORGANIZED AND LED THEM:

NATO IN WESTERN EUROPE,
ANZUS IN THE SOUTH PACIFIC,
SEATO IN SOUTHEAST ASIA.

THE U.S. WAS NOW THE WORLD'S
FOREMOST MILITARY POWER !!

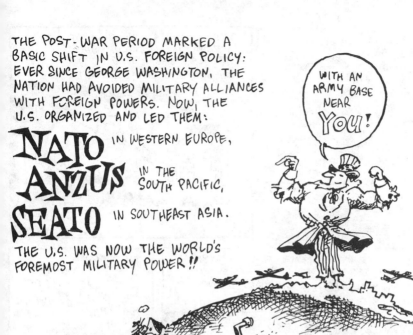

THE WARTIME
ALLIANCE WITH
RUSSIA WAS
REINTERPRETED IN
THE NEW SCHEME
OF THINGS:
THERE MUST BE
**COMMUNIST
SYMPATHIZERS**
IN GOVERNMENT!
ROOSEVELT HAD
LOST POLAND!!
THE COMMUNIST PARTY
WAS A **FIFTH
COLUMN !!** NEVER
MIND RUSSIA —
WHAT ABOUT
COMMUNISM **WITHIN?**

IN 1946, A GAGGLE OF REPUBLICANS (INCLUDING RICHARD NIXON) RODE THE COMMUNISM ISSUE INTO CONGRESS.

...AND THE U.S., WITH ONE OF THE WORLD'S SMALLEST COMMUNIST PARTIES, BEGAN ONE OF THE WORLD'S BIGGEST RED HUNTS.

COMMUNISTS WERE BLAMED FOR THE STRIKE WAVE OF '46 AND '47 — THE BIGGEST IN AMERICAN HISTORY. EVEN WALT DISNEY PRODUCTIONS WENT ON STRIKE!!

NATIONAL SECURITY IS THREATENED!!

THE HOUSE UNAMERICAN ACTIVITIES COMMITTEE DESCENDED ON HOLLYWOOD

NOW PLAYING "ARE YOU NOW OR HAVE YOU EVER BEEN?"

THE CIO DEMANDED THAT MEMBER UNIONS EJECT THEIR COMMUNISTS, EVEN FREELY ELECTED OFFICIALS. IF NOT, THE CIO EJECTED THE UNION.

AND OUT GOES DEMOCRACY!

THE RESULT WAS THE BLACKLIST, THE LOYALTY OATH, BURGLARIES & HARASSMENT BY THE FBI, AND FOR MANY, JAIL TERMS FOR "CONSPIRING TO TEACH" MARXISM!

124

WAS THE "YEAR OF SHOCKS."

SHOCK #1: THE U.S.S.R. EXPLODED AN ATOMIC BOMB.

SHOCK #2: THE CHINESE REVOLUTION BROUGHT THE COMMUNISTS TO POWER.

CHINESE REDS WIN!

REMIND ME TO STOP READING THE PAPER...

PARANOIA SWELLED...

WHO LOST CHINA?

WHO GAVE AWAY THE BOMB?

WHO ATTACKED MICKEY MOUSE?

THEY DID!!

ENTER SENATOR JOE McCARTHY...

GET 'EM, JOE!!

McCARTHY'S ANTI-COMMUNISM WAS HARDLY DIFFERENT FROM THAT OF NIXON ET AL.... BUT HE SURPASSED THEM ALL IN DISHONESTY AND FLAIR... McCARTHY'S ROLE WAS TO MAKE THE WILDEST CHARGES OF SUBVERSION... BULLY WITNESSES AND CRITICS THE MOST RUDELY... WHIP UP PARANOIA THE MOST INTENSELY... HE WAS HORRIBLE... HE GOT LOTS OF PRESS... AND, AS HE CAST HYSTERICAL SUSPICION ON ALL DEMOCRATS, HE WAS TOLERATED BY HIS REPUBLICAN COLLEAGUES.

IT WAS AT THIS RELAXING MOMENT THAT THE NORTH KOREAN COMMUNISTS DECIDED TO INVADE SOUTH KOREA.

THE U.S. SENT IN TROOPS... THEY MARCHED UNDER A U.N. FLAG, TO KEEP UP APPEARANCES, BUT THEIR COMMANDER, GEN. DOUGLAS MACARTHUR, ANSWERED ONLY TO WASHINGTON.

GOT US SOME "GOOKS," LEROY!

AS THE WAR CRUNCHED UP AND DOWN THE KOREAN PENINSULA, THE AMERICAN PARADOX BECAME CLEARER... TO "DEFEND DEMOCRACY" IT WAS NECESSARY TO PROP UP A CORRUPT DICTATOR, SYNGMAN RHEE... REFUSE ELECTIONS (THE COMMIES MIGHT WIN!)... AND BOMB EVERY "TARGET" (I.E., TOWN) IN KOREA INTO RUBBLE!

127

WITH WORLD WAR III LOOMING, TENSION ROSE...

MCCARTHY BLAMED THE KOREAN WAR ON THE EARLIER "SOFTNESS" OF THE "COMMIECRAT" PARTY.

I AIN'T SAYIN' THEY'RE ALL SPIES, NECESSARILY.

HEY, WE CAN SHOW AS MUCH CONTEMPT FOR THE CONSTITUTION AS ANYONE!

YES, BE FAIR!

SO THE DEMOCRATS VIED WITH MCCARTHY TO ESTABLISH THEIR ANTI-COMMUNIST CREDENTIALS.

WHEN THE REPUBLICANS INTRODUCED AN "INTERNAL SECURITY ACT," LIBERAL DEMOCRATS ADDED AN AMENDMENT CREATING CONCENTRATION CAMPS FOR SUSPECTED COMMUNISTS... ULTRALIBERAL HUBERT HUMPHREY DRAFTED A LAW DECLARING THE COMMUNIST PARTY TO BE NO PARTY AT ALL, BUT A CRIMINAL CONSPIRACY!!

TOUGH ENOUGH?

NEVERTHELESS, '52 BROUGHT A REPUBLICAN INTO THE WHITE HOUSE, WAR HERO DWIGHT D. EISENHOWER.

"IKE'S" VEEP WAS NIXON, SMARTEST OF THE McCARTHYITE GROUP.

SECRETARY OF STATE WAS THE PIOUSLY ANTI-COMMUNIST JOHN FOSTER DULLES.

IN '53 THEY ENDED THE KOREAN WAR.

IN '54 McCARTHY WAS SILENCED...

...AND, OVERTLY AT LEAST, PEACE FELL...

DRINK?

WHILE, COVERTLY, DULLES'S LITTLE BROTHER ALLEN WAS LEADING THE CENTRAL INTELLIGENCE AGENCY INTO SOME NEW ARENAS: ASSASSINATION, PSY-WAR, LSD EXPERIMENTS.

OUR STRATEGIC SUPPLY OF BANANAS IS IMPERILED!

THE CIA BECAME AN ACTIVE FOREIGN POLICY ARM, SECRETLY AIDING THE OVERTHROW OF LEFTIST—THOUGH ELECTED—GOVERNMENTS IN IRAN AND GUATEMALA.

AND SO... UNTROUBLED
BY DANGEROUS THOUGHTS,
AMERICANS SET ABOUT
ENJOYING THEIR NEW
SUPERPOWER STATUS...
GROSS NATIONAL PRODUCT
CLIMBED YEAR AFTER
YEAR... TRACT HOUSING
SPROUTED LIKE CRABGRASS
IN THE SUBURBS...
THE TAILFIN WAS
INVENTED IN '55... AT
LAST, THE AMERICAN
DREAM WAS COMING
TRUE !!!

SO WHAT IF THE TRACT HOUSE HAD A BACK-YARD BOMB SHELTER FULL OF SALTINES?

OR IF SCHOOL KIDS WERE DUCKING UNDER THEIR DESKS IN AIR-RAID DRILLS THAT NO ONE BELIEVED WOULD PROTECT THEM FROM THE BOMB?

HANDS OVER OUR NECKS, CLASS! IT'S IMPORTANT TO VAPORIZE OUR HANDS FIRST!

OR IF MOM WAS BECOMING AN ISOLATED BEING-IN-A-BOX?

M-I-C-K-E-Y...

OR IF PUBLIC HOUSING LOOKED LIKE THIS?

OR IF, WHEN 112 PEOPLE WERE ASKED TO SIGN A PETITION ENDORSING THE DECLARATION OF INDEPENDENCE, 111 REFUSED?

OR IF BLACKS STILL RODE THE BACK OF THE BUS?

OR IF THE INDUSTRIAL BOOM DEPENDED ON CHURNING OUT PRODUCTS NOBODY NEEDED — OR EVEN IMAGINED BEFORE?

FABRIC SOFTENER?

131

ONE LITTLE THING DISTURBED THIS PEACEFUL SCENE...
A LITTLE SATELLITE CALLED SPUTNIK...
THE FIRST SUCCESSFUL ROCKET-LAUNCHED
ARTIFICIAL MOON—AND IT
WAS **RUSSIAN!**

UNTIL 1945, THE WORLD'S BEST ROCKET
PROGRAM WAS IN GERMANY.
AFTER THE WAR, THE U.S.
AND U.S.S.R. DIVIDED UP THE
GERMAN SCIENTISTS,
REGARDLESS OF POLITICAL
AFFILIATION OR WAR
CRIMES.   NOW, WITH
SPUTNIK, THE TRUTH
BECAME CLEAR!!

THEIR GERMANS ARE BETTER THAN OUR GERMANS!

THIS WAS NO MERE QUESTION OF NATIONAL PRIDE.

IT WAS OBVIOUS TO EVERYONE THAT YOU COULD EQUIP THESE MISSILES WITH H-BOMBS IN THEIR NOSES... THE RUSSIANS WERE SUDDENLY CAPABLE OF DELIVERING ANNIHILATION TO YOUR BACK YARD IN ABOUT HALF AN HOUR.

BUT IF POLITICAL PROTEST WAS MUTED, STILL, UNDER THE MINDLESS MARCH OF CONFORMITY, SOMETHING WAS BUBBLING...

...AMONG SOUTHERN BLACKS, WHO HAD BEGUN TO CHALLENGE SEGREGATION WITH LAWSUITS AND BOYCOTTS...

...AMONG ALIENATED WHITE (AND BLACK) POETS AND DRIFTERS, WHO GATHERED IN COFFEEHOUSES WITH BONGOS AND BLACK TURTLENECKS...

CIVIL RIGHTS LAWYER THURGOOD MARSHALL

LIKE.. EXISTEN IS SO... SO... SO WHAT?

SO VERY, VERY WHAT..

JUST ABOUT THE ONLY SIGNS OF
CULTURAL VITALITY WERE OUTSIDE
THE MAINSTREAM... LIKE THE
ANGRY PROSE OF JAMES BALDWIN...

THE
ESOTERIC BEBOP OF
PARKER, GILLESPIE, MONK...

THE POETRY OF ALLEN GINSBERG,
PROSECUTED FOR OBSCENITY...

HOWL

SHOULD
HAVE BEEN
FOR
OBSCURITY!

SATIRE LIKE
KELLY'S "POGO"...

OR THE INSPIRED
PARODIES OF KURTZMAN'S

MAD.

IT WAS ALSO THE "GOLDEN AGE" OF
TV... THIS WAS IN THE MAINSTREAM,
BUT HOW EXCITED CAN YOU GET
ABOUT MILTON BERLE IN DRAG?

135

AND... AND... WHAT
WAS WITH THOSE

TEENAGERS?

WHAT WERE THEY LISTENING TO?
IT WAS AMAZINGLY LIKE THE 1920's ALL
OVER AGAIN: GOVERNMENT MIND CONTROL
WAS FAILING TO TAKE HOLD BELOW THE
BELT!! ONCE AGAIN, BLACK DANCE MUSIC
WAS CROSSING OVER: FATS DOMINO, CHUCK
BERRY, LITTLE RICHARD... AND THE
MESSAGE WAS... SEXY!

THEN CAME ELVIS, THE WHITE KID WHO COULD "SING BLACK," AND **ROCK 'N' ROLL** WENT **OUT OF CONTROL!**

AND SO, BETWEEN THE "RESPECTABLE" PARENTS AND THEIR CHILDREN, A GENERATION GAP OPENED UP...

137

MEANWHILE, BACK IN THE REAL WORLD, SOMETHING WAS HAPPENING THAT AFFECTED THE '60's AND EVERYTHING AFTERWARD:

DECOLONIZATION.

REMEMBER: UNTIL 1945, SEVERAL WESTERN EUROPEAN COUNTRIES WERE MORE THAN COUNTRIES — THEY WERE HEADS OF EMPIRES.

BRITAIN RULED
INDIA
BURMA
SUDAN
KENYA
UGANDA
RHODESIA
ETC ETC ETC...

PIP PIP

FRANCE RULED
ALGERIA
TUNISIA
VIETNAM
CAMBODIA
LAOS
CHAD
ETC ETC ETC...

BIEN SUR!

THE NETHERLANDS RULED INDONESIA; BELGIUM HAD THE CONGO; PORTUGAL OWNED ANGOLA, MOZAMBIQUE, GOA...

AS AMERICA VAGUELY REMEMBERED, BEING A COLONY WAS NO FUN.

OH, YEAH...

AND, LIKE AMERICA IN 1776, QUITE A FEW OF THESE 20TH-CENTURY COLONIES HAD INDEPENDENCE MOVEMENTS!

B-BUT— THEY'RE NOT WH-WHITE!

AFTER WORLD WAR II, SOME OF THESE MOVEMENTS SUCCEEDED, BEGINNING WITH THE INDEPENDENCE OF

INDIA + PAKISTAN (1947)
BURMA ('48)
VIETNAM + CAMBODIA ('55)
INDONESIA ('55)
SUDAN ('56)

CHAPTER 8

REVOLUTION NOW?

AS BRITAIN, FRANCE, HOLLAND, AND CO. WITHDREW FROM THEIR OVERSEAS POSSESSIONS, THE UNITED STATES OFTEN STEPPED IN.

THIS WAS CALLED neo-COLONIALISM, BECAUSE, ALTHOUGH THE COUNTRIES RETAINED NOMINAL INDEPENDENCE, THEIR POLICIES WERE SUBJECT TO U.S. PRIORITIES.

YOU CAN KEEP THE FLAG!

POLICE TRAINING

ECONOMIC ADVISERS

FOREIGN AID

CIA

AND WOE TO THE COUNTRY THAT SHOWED REAL INDEPENDENCE!

FOR TWO EXAMPLES:

VIETNAM

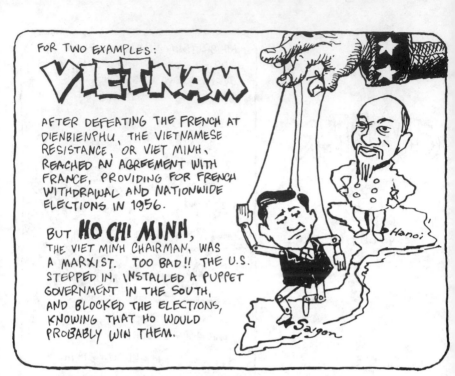

AFTER DEFEATING THE FRENCH AT DIENBIENPHU, THE VIETNAMESE RESISTANCE, OR VIET MINH, REACHED AN AGREEMENT WITH FRANCE, PROVIDING FOR FRENCH WITHDRAWAL AND NATIONWIDE ELECTIONS IN 1956.

BUT **HO CHI MINH**, THE VIET MINH CHAIRMAN, WAS A MARXIST. TOO BAD!! THE U.S. STEPPED IN, INSTALLED A PUPPET GOVERNMENT IN THE SOUTH, AND BLOCKED THE ELECTIONS, KNOWING THAT HO WOULD PROBABLY WIN THEM.

CUBA,

NOMINALLY INDEPENDENT, WAS IN FACT MORE OR LESS WHOLLY OWNED BY THE U.S.A. IN '59, **FIDEL CASTRO** LED A REVOLUTION WITH OTHER IDEAS... IT WASN'T EVEN KNOWN AT THE TIME IF CASTRO WAS A COMMUNIST— BUT HE THREATENED U.S. ECONOMIC INTERESTS, SO THE C I A BEGAN PLOTTING AGAINST HIM...

ANOTHER INGREDIENT
IN THE SOON-TO-BE-BUBBLING
BREW OF THE '60's WAS THE

CIVIL RIGHTS MOVEMENT.

AFTER WORLD WAR II, THE GOVERNMENT
REALIZED THAT RACISM WAS
A BLOT ON AMERICA'S IMAGE
AS WORLD LEADER... SO
BARRIERS AGAINST BLACKS
BEGAN COMING DOWN.

¿AHEM¿
WE'RE DOING THE
BEST WE CAN!
AND WE'VE BEEN
DOING IT FOR
MANY, MANY
MONTHS!

WHITES ONLY

WHITES ONLY

THE FIRST COLOR BARRIER TO FALL,
IN 1947, WAS IN MAJOR-LEAGUE
BASEBALL. NEXT, IN '48,
TRUMAN ORDERED
THE MILITARY
DESEGREGATED...

...AND THE SUPREME COURT
ISSUED A SERIES OF ANTI-
DISCRIMINATION RULINGS,
MOST NOTABLY **BROWN** vs.
BOARD OF EDUCATION,
BANNING SEGREGATED
PUBLIC SCHOOLS.

141

THE COURT RULED THAT SEGREGATION MUST FALL "WITH ALL DELIBERATE SPEED." THIS WAS OPEN TO INTERPRETATION, ESPECIALLY DOWN SOUTH,* WHERE BLACKS EMPHASIZED THE SPEED, WHILE WHITES STRESSED DELIBERATION.

WE DEE-LIBERATIN' AS DEE-LIBERATELY AS WE CAN...

MONTGOMERY, ALA., WAS TYPICAL: BY LAW, BLACKS SAT IN THE BACK OF THE BUS — UNTIL A WHITE PERSON DEMANDED A SEAT, WHEN THEY STOOD...

...UNTIL DEC. 1, 1955, WHEN CIVIL RIGHTS ACTIVIST *ROSA PARKS* SAID NO...

PARKS WAS PUT OFF THE BUS, ARRESTED, AND JAILED.

THIS SPARKED THE *MONTGOMERY BUS BOYCOTT*, THE FIRST DIRECT ACTION OF THE CIVIL RIGHTS MOVEMENT. FOR A YEAR, BLACKS WALKED AND CARPOOLED, ENDURING HEAT, HARASS-MENT, THREATS, JAIL, AND EVEN BOMBS — AND WON VICTORY WITH A SUPREME COURT RULING AGAINST MONTGOMERY'S SEGREGATED BUSES.

* BUT NOT ONLY IN THE SOUTH. FOR EXAMPLE, THE ARMY TOOK YEARS TO INTEGRATE FULLY, WHILE THE AIR FORCE DID IT IN ONE DAY.

THE BOYCOTT'S LEADER WAS A 27-YEAR-OLD MINISTER,

MARTIN LUTHER KING, JR.,

AN EXCEPTIONAL COMBINATION OF BRAVERY, VISION, ELOQUENCE, MORAL FORCE, AND TACTICAL KNOW-HOW. WHEN HIS HOUSE WAS BOMBED, KING DISPERSED AN ANGRY CROWD OF BLACKS WITH THESE WORDS:

WE MUST MEET VIOLENCE WITH NON-VIOLENCE.

WHO'S NON-VIOLENT?

KING THEN ORGANIZED THE *SOUTHERN CHRISTIAN LEADERSHIP CONFERENCE* TO CONTINUE NON-VIOLENT DIRECT ACTION.

TENSION ROSE IN THE SOUTH, AND FBI CHIEF J. EDGAR HOOVER DECIDED THAT KING WAS SOME KIND OF SUBVERSIVE.

AND I HAVE TAPE RECORDINGS OF HIS SEX LIFE TO PROVE IT!

143

1960: IKE BOWS OUT WITH AN ASTONISHING WARNING AGAINST AMERICA'S GROWING "MILITARY-INDUSTRIAL COMPLEX"... AND IN COMES A YOUNG, VIGOROUS, AND CHARMING BOSTONIAN,

JOHN F. KENNEDY.

(HIS OPPONENT, NIXON, FORGETS TO POWDER HIS 5 O'CLOCK SHADOW ON TV, AND LOSES THE ELECTION BY A WHISKER.)

GRRR

"ASK NOT WHAT YOUR COUNTRY CAN DO FOR YOU, BUT WHAT YOU CAN DO FOR YOUR COUNTRY."

KENNEDY APPEALS TO YOUNG AMERICANS' IDEALISM. HE CALLS HIS PROGRAM THE **NEW FRONTIER**.

AND THEY RESPOND, SOME BY JOINING THE PEACE CORPS AND SEEING THE WORLD... OTHERS BY JOINING THE CIVIL RIGHTS MOVEMENT AND SEEING THE SOUTH.

144

IN 1963, CIVIL RIGHTS DEMONSTRATIONS TOOK PLACE IN 186 CITIES ACROSS THE COUNTRY... A BLACK STUDENT ENROLLED AT THE UNIVERSITY OF ALABAMA...SEGREGATION RECEDED... IN JUNE, KENNEDY PROPOSED A CIVIL RIGHTS ACT TO CONGRESS ... IN AUGUST, 250,000 PEOPLE MARCHED PEACEFULLY TO WASHINGTON, WHERE MARTIN LUTHER KING GAVE HIS FAMOUS SPEECH...

"I HAVE A DREAM THAT ONE DAY ON THE RED HILLS OF GEORGIA THE SONS OF FORMER SLAVES AND THE SONS OF FORMER SLAVE OWNERS WILL BE ABLE TO SIT DOWN TOGETHER AT THE TABLE OF BROTHERHOOD..."

MEANWHILE, IN CUBA, KENNEDY CARRIED OUT EISENHOWER'S PLAN: IN 1961, CIA-TRAINED CUBANS INVADED THE ISLAND'S BAY OF PIGS AND WAITED FOR THE MASSES TO RISE UP AND EMBRACE THEM. DREAM ON!!

THE CIA TURNED TO MORE EXOTIC IDEAS, WHILE CASTRO TURNED TO THE USSR FOR MILITARY AID.

RUSSIA SENT BALLISTIC MISSILES... KENNEDY SENT THE NAVY TO CONFRONT THE RUSSIAN CONVOY... FOR SEVERAL DAYS THE WORLD TEETERED ON THE BRINK...

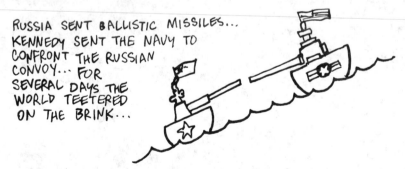

FINALLY, THE CRISIS ENDED WHEN THE USSR AGREED TO WITHDRAW THE MISSILES AND THE U.S. PROMISED TO LEAVE CASTRO IN PEACE.

146

AND IN SOUTH VIETNAM, A MESS: SAIGON, THE CAPITAL, A VAST SLUM... LAND REFORM IN THE HANDS OF A LANDLORD... GROWING OPPOSITION TO DIEM'S CORRUPT GOVERNMENT...

KENNEDY, CONCLUDING THAT DIEM WAS NO LONGER USEFUL, GAVE THE NOD, AND THE VIETNAMESE PRESIDENT WAS ASSASSINATED ON NOV. 1, 1963.

THREE WEEKS LATER, THE AMERICAN PRESIDENT WAS ASSASSINATED...

A FEW DAYS LATER, KENNEDY'S ASSASSIN WAS ASSASSINATED, ON LIVE TV — AND NOW THE '60'S HAD REALLY BEGUN...

THE SAME DAY KENNEDY WAS SHOT, TWO OF MY HIGH-SCHOOL FRIENDS — 16 AND 17 YEARS OLD (!!) — TOOK PEYOTE* FOR THE FIRST TIME. THEY HAD VISIONS OF EVIL UNLEASHED.

HOME-MADE THELONIOUS MONK SWEATSHIRTS

LET'S LOOSEN OUR NECKTIES...

PSYCHEDELIC DRUGS HAD HIT THE MEDIA THE PREVIOUS YEAR, WHEN HARVARD'S TIMOTHY LEARY WAS FIRED FOR TURNING ON TO L S D WITH HIS STUDENTS.

BY '65, A DRUG CULTURE AROSE, COMPLETE WITH A FABRIC (PAISLEY), A MUSIC (ACID ROCK), AND AN OFFICIAL OUTBURST:

OH, WOW!

* THEN LEGALLY AVAILABLE FROM A TEXAS CACTUS FARM.

148

UNAWARE OF THIS
DISTURBANCE IN THE
PSYCHIC ATMOSPHERE,
VICE PRESIDENT

LYNDON JOHNSON

TOOK THE OATH OF
OFFICE.

THE TALL TEXAN FULFILLED KENNEDY'S PROMISE WITH
FIVE YEARS OF STRONG CIVIL RIGHTS AND SOCIAL
LEGISLATION.

THE CIVIL RIGHTS ACT

THE VOTING RIGHTS ACT

FOOD STAMPS

MEDICARE

OFFICE OF ECONOMIC
OPPORTUNITY

OCCUPATIONAL SAFETY AND
HEALTH ADMINISTRATION

THE WAR ON POVERTY

UNFORTUNATELY, THE WAR
ON POVERTY WASN'T
JOHNSON'S ONLY WAR...

PAUSING BRIEFLY TO CELEBRATE A LANDSLIDE ELECTION VICTORY ON A PEACE PLATFORM, JOHNSON NOW BEGAN SENDING GROUND TROOPS TO VIETNAM.

JOHNSON'S STRATEGISTS WERE "THE BEST AND THE BRIGHTEST," INTELLECTUALS WHO UNDERSTOOD THE SUBTLETIES OF DEFENDING DEMOCRACY IN A COUNTRY WHERE YOU HAD REFUSED TO HOLD ELECTIONS.

THEIR POLYSYLLABIC PREFERENCES PERHAPS PROMOTED THE PENTAGON'S PENCHANT FOR PRETENTIOUS PROSE. FOR EXAMPLE:

TRI-CIRCUMVOLUTORY TRANSLOCATION DEVICE

"STRATEGIC HAMLET PROGRAM" (UPROOTING VILLAGERS AND MOVING THEM TO CAMPS)

"PROTECTIVE REACTION" ("REACTING" TO SOMETHING THAT HADN'T HAPPENED YET)

"SURGICAL BOMBING" (BOMBING)

"ANTI-PERSONNEL DEVICE" (NAPALM, WHITE PHOSPHORUS, FRAGMENTATION GRENADES)

"PACIFICATION" (KILLING AND TORTURE)

UP THE ESCALATOR

IN 1964, THE U.S. HAD 20,000 "MILITARY ADVISERS"* IN SOUTH VIETNAM, PROPPING UP DIEM'S SUCCESSOR. THE OPPOSITION NATIONAL LIBERATION FRONT, SUPPORTED BY THE NORTH, WAGED A GUERRILLA WAR, AND THEY SEEMED TO BE ON THE VERGE OF WINNING.

ON AUG. 5, JOHNSON ACCUSED NORTH VIETNAM OF ATTACKING U.S. SHIPS IN THE GULF OF TONKIN. ON AUG. 7, CONGRESS PASSED THE "TONKIN GULF RESOLUTION," A BLANK CHECK FOR JOHNSON TO DO "WHATEVER IS NECESSARY..."

PAY TO THE ORDER OF Lyndon Johnson THE AMOUNT OF:

AND JOHNSON BEGAN TO BOMB NORTH VIETNAM — 2 DAYS BEFORE THE RESOLUTION WAS PASSED !!

* MOSTLY HELICOPTER PILOTS.

BERKELEY, 1964. THE FIRST BIG STUDENT DEMONSTRATION: THE **FREE SPEECH MOVEMENT** PROTESTS A UNIVERSITY BAN ON "POLITICAL TABLES" ON THE CAMPUS PLAZA.

COALITION POLITICS.

SEXUAL FREEDOM LEAGUE

FSM

CIVIL RIGHTS VETERANS FOUNDED THE **S**TUDENTS FOR A **D**EMOCRATIC **S**OCIETY (SDS) TO SPONSOR ANTI-WAR "TEACH-INS" AND DEMONSTRATIONS. DRAFT CARDS BURNED TO THE SMOLDERING CHANT OF "GIRLS SAY YES TO BOYS WHO SAY NO."

AS LONG AS WE'RE HAVING A REVOLUTION, MIGHT AS WELL MAKE IT A SEXUAL REVOLUTION!

FOOSH

MEANWHILE, BLACKS WERE LOSING PATIENCE WITH WHITE RACISM... THE VIETNAM WAR DEVOURED THEM...

ELIJAH MOHAMMED,

PREACHING THAT WHITES ARE DEVILS, ATTRACTED MANY BLACKS TO HIS MUSLIM SECT. THE MESSAGE WAS "BLACK IS BEAUTIFUL"... THE AFRO EXPANDED...

BUT THE MUSLIMS' MOST ELOQUENT SPEAKER,

MALCOLM X,

HAD A VISION OF RACIAL HARMONY ON A TRIP TO MECCA. HE BROKE WITH ELIJAH MOHAMMED... AND IN 1965, MALCOLM X WAS ASSASSINATED.

...BY THE MUSLIMS? BY THE CIA? BY MUSLIMS WHO WERE CIA? NO ONE KNOWS...

IN '66 THE SWELLING RAGE BROKE IN THE TIDAL WAVE OF LOS ANGELES'S WATTS RIOTS. FINAL TOLL: 40 DEAD, HUNDREDS OF ACRES CHARRED.

WHY YOU WANNA BURN DOWN THE NEIGHBORHOOD?

AIN'T YOU NEVER HEARD OF URBAN RENEWAL?

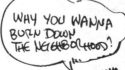

153

3 POWERS OF 1967:

FIRE POWER: 400,000 G.I.'S (DISPROPORTIONATELY BLACK) IN "THE NAM," TRYING TO WIN VIETNAMESE HEARTS & MINDS WHILE WASTING THEIR COUNTRY... FOR THE G.I., A YEAR OF HELL... FOR THE VIETNAMESE, MORE THAN A YEAR.

M-60 M GUN...

BLACK POWER: ERUPTIONS IN THE GHETTOS OF DETROIT, NEWARK, ETC. ETC. ETC... THE CHANT OF "BURN, BABY, BURN..." POLICE SHOOTING TO KILL... THEIR FIRE RETURNED... MORE LIKE A REVOLT THAN A RIOT!

FLOWER POWER: IN SAN FRANCISCO, THE "SUMMER OF LOVE" (??!!)... HIPPIES, BIKERS, BLACK PANTHERS, THE FARM, THE FAMILY, THE FAMILY DOG... PAINTED FACES, ACID ROCK, THE LOVE-IN, THE BE-IN, SPEED, ACID, GRASS...

(WITH APOLOGIES TO R. CRUMB AND GILBERT SHELTON)

154

 (SHUDDER!), AN ELECTION YEAR... 550,000 AMERICANS IN VIETNAM... MASSIVE BOMBING OF THE NORTH...

THINGS AIN'T GOIN' ACCORDIN' TO PLAN.

U.S. SOLDIERS MASSACRE MORE THAN 400 WOMEN AND CHILDREN AT MY LAI... MARTIN LUTHER KING SPEAKS OUT AGAINST THE WAR... THE DEMOCRATS BEGIN TO DESERT JOHNSON... HE ANNOUNCES THAT HE WON'T RUN AGAIN... HE EASES THE BOMBING... PEACE TALKS BEGIN... SEVERAL ANTI-WAR CANDIDATES EMERGE, INCLUDING ROBERT KENNEDY, JOHN'S YOUNGER BROTHER.

ON APRIL 4, MARTIN LUTHER KING IS SHOT...

IN JUNE, ROBERT KENNEDY FALLS...

AT THE DEMOCRATIC CONVENTION IN CHICAGO, THE POLICE ATTACK DEMONSTRATORS... MIRACULOUSLY, NO ONE IS KILLED.

CALL US PIGS, WILL YOU?

156

BUT IN NOVEMBER, THE CANDIDATES WERE: PRO-WAR DEMOCRAT HUBERT HUMPHREY, ALABAMA GOV. GEORGE WALLACE (WHOSE CAMPAIGN HAD FASCIST OVERTONES), AND THE WINNER, WITH 43% OF THE POPULAR VOTE.........??!!

HI!! I'M BACK!

NIXON CLAIMED TO HAVE A "SECRET PLAN" TO END THE WAR...

THE PLAN, "OPERATION DUCK HOOK," WAS TO MAKE A SERIES OF ESCALATING THREATS AGAINST NORTH VIETNAM, CULMINATING, IF NECESSARY, IN THE USE OF NUKES. IN NOV., '69, NIXON SECRETLY* PUT U.S. FORCES ON FULL NUCLEAR ALERT.

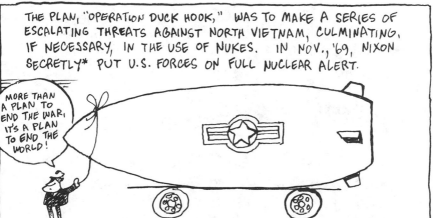

MORE THAN A PLAN TO END THE WAR, IT'S A PLAN TO END THE WORLD!

BEFORE SEEING HOW THIS TURNED OUT, LET'S NOTE A COUPLE OF OTHER EVENTS FROM 1969.

AN AMERICAN, NEIL ARMSTRONG, LANDED ON THE MOON...

ANOTHER AMERICAN, CHARLES MANSON, PROGRAMMED TEEN-AGE GIRLS WITH LSD TO COMMIT POINT-LESS, GRUESOME MURDERS.

* THAT IS, IT WAS A SECRET FROM THE AMERICAN PEOPLE, MOST OF WHOM PROBABLY THOUGHT THAT NIXON WAS SIMPLY LYING ABOUT HAVING A PLAN. THE SOVIET GOVERNMENT, HOWEVER, WAS KEPT FULLY INFORMED!

NIXON'S ESCALATION BEGAN:
HE MINED HAIPHONG HARBOR;
BOMBED NORTH VIETNAM'S
IRRIGATION DIKES; AND
EVENTUALLY WASTED THE
LITTLE COUNTRY WITH MORE
EXPLOSIVE POWER THAN ALL
THE BOMBS OF WORLD WAR II.

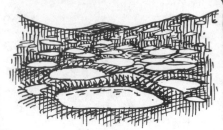

250,000 PROTESTERS
DESCENDED ON
WASHINGTON...
THE OUTCRY WAS
SO LOUD THAT
NIXON BACKED
OFF THE NUCLEAR
OPTION.

AS THE WAR DRAGGED ON — AND WIDENED INTO
CAMBODIA AND LAOS — IT BEGAN TO LOOK LIKE
WAR AT HOME... BOMBS DEMOLISHED BANKS,
COMPUTER CENTERS, ROTC BUILDINGS...

THE FBI GUNNED
DOWN BLACK RADICALS
IN BED...GUARDSMEN
KILLED STUDENTS
AT KENT STATE
(OHIO) AND
JACKSON STATE
(MISSISSIPPI).

158

IN 1971, A DISGRUNTLED
PENTAGON ANALYST,
DANIEL ELLSBERG,
LEAKED THE
"PENTAGON PAPERS"
TO THE PRESS,
DOCUMENTING
GOVERNMENT LIES
AND SELF-DECEPTION
ON VIETNAM.
THE PUBLIC WAS
ALMOST AS AGHAST
AS THE PRESIDENT!

NIXON CREATED THE "PLUMBERS," A SECRET TEAM TO
PLUG LEAKS. THEY BURGLED ELLSBERG'S PSYCHIATRIST'S
OFFICE, VAINLY SEEKING SOMETHING TO SMEAR HIM WITH.

THEN—AS THE '72 ELECTIONS DREW NEAR, THE
PLUMBERS WERE CAUGHT TAPPING PHONES IN THE
DEMOCRATS' HEADQUARTERS AT THE WATERGATE
APARTMENT COMPLEX IN WASHINGTON, D.C.

BUT NIXON ESCAPED RESPONSIBILITY UNTIL AFTER THE ELECTION, WHICH HE WON BY A LANDSLIDE — AND THEN THE AMAZING STORY CAME OUT:

* THE EXISTENCE OF THE PLUMBERS

* THE ELLSBERG BURGLARY

* "ENEMIES" HARASSED BY THE IRS AND BEATEN BY THUGS

* THE ATTORNEY GENERAL'S PRIOR KNOWLEDGE

* SUITCASEFULS OF $100 BILLS FOR "HUSH MONEY"

* AN INTERNATIONAL MONEY-LAUNDERING OPERATION

* MASSIVE INFLUENCE-PEDDLING

* A COVER-UP INVOLVING THE FBI, CIA, + WHITE HOUSE...

SAID NIXON.

... AND THE MOST INCREDIBLE THING: A SECRET WHITE HOUSE TAPING SYSTEM, RECORDING IT ALL FOR POSTERITY!!

THIS IS ☆◎#✳ ✻$@ HISTORY, BOB!

☆✳·⋸# RIGHT, BOSS!

(EIGHTEEN CRUCIAL MINUTES HAD BEEN ERASED, THOUGH... TOO BAD!)

NOT A CROOK... NOT A CROOK... NOT A CROOK...

FACING IMPEACHMENT, NIXON RESIGNED IN 1974. HIS TOP AIDES, AN ATTORNEY GENERAL OR TWO, AND A SLEW OF JUNIOR ASSISTANTS WENT TO JAIL — AN AMERICAN FIRST!

HE'S A CROOK! HE'S A CROOK!

...BUT BEFORE RETIRING, NIXON "VIETNAMIZED" THE WAR — I.E., TURNED THE FIGHTING OVER TO THE SOUTH VIETNAMESE ARMY.

JUST REMIND ME WHAT WE'RE FIGHTING FOR...?

WHERE'S THE DAMN TICKER TAPE?

...AND THE AMERICAN BOYS FINALLY CAME HOME (ALTHOUGH CAPTURED PILOTS RETURNED LATER).

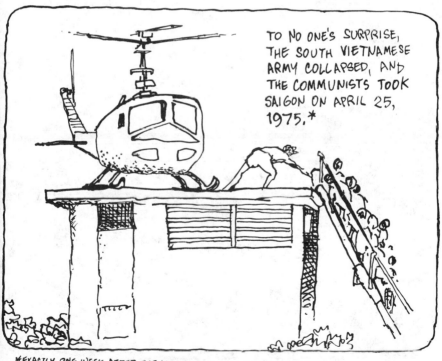

TO NO ONE'S SURPRISE, THE SOUTH VIETNAMESE ARMY COLLAPSED, AND THE COMMUNISTS TOOK SAIGON ON APRIL 25, 1975.*

*EXACTLY ONE WEEK AFTER THE KICK-OFF OF THE U.S. BICENTENNIAL.

1960:

1975:

CHAPTER 9
AND THEY LIVED HAPPILY EVER AFTER

READING THAT LAST
CHAPTER, YOU MIGHT WELL
WONDER **WHAT
WAS SO GREAT
ABOUT THE
SIXTIES?**

ALL THAT BLOOD AND
GUTS — WHAT'S TO BE
NOSTALGIC ABOUT?

NOSTALGIC?
WHY, ARE THEY
OVER?

WELL, I LIVED THROUGH IT — LET'S SEE IF I CAN DUST OFF MY BRAIN CELLS AND REMEMBER...

"PICTURE YOURSELF ON A BOAT ON A RIVER..." THE MUSIC, OF COURSE!! NOT JUST THE BEATLES & STONES, BUT THE SOUL SOURCE: THE TEMPTATIONS, THE IMPRESSIONS, THE MIRACLES, JAMES BROWN, ARETHA FRANKLIN, WILSON PICKETT, RAY CHARLES...

BIRTH CONTROL PILLS... THEY MADE THE SEXUAL REVOLUTION POSSIBLE.

MYSTIC ECSTACY AT THE DROP OF A "TAB"... A SENSE THAT ANYTHING WAS POSSIBLE... COMMUNAL LIVING... FREE FOOD... A LOOSENING... AN INFORMALITY... HITCHHIKING WAS COMMON... TELEPHONE OPERATORS (IN L.A.) WOULD CHAT AIMLESSLY AS LONG AS YOU LIKED!!

FAR OUT!

165

SOME UNPLEASANT '60'S SIDE EFFECTS ARE STILL WITH US — DRUGS, FOR EXAMPLE. THE POST-'60's GENERATION WENT FOR COCAINE, TO BUILD CONFIDENCE, AND PCP, FOR THAT DELIGHTFUL SENSATION OF BEING A RAMPAGING BULL ELEPHANT.

ROCK 'N' ROLL!

DON'T FORGET THE ASSASSINATION FAD—BOTH GOVERNMENT-SPONSORED AND FREE-LANCE.

THE SEXUAL REVOLUTION, WHEN COMBINED WITH A TRADITIONAL PURITAN RESISTANCE TO SEX EDUCATION, CREATED THE WORLD'S HIGHEST TEEN PREGNANCY RATE AND SPREAD VARIOUS VENEREAL DISEASES, MOST RECENTLY THE DREAD

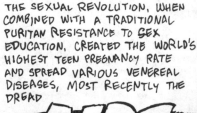

AIDS.

A FLOWERING OF CULTS, FROM THE BENIGN TO THE RIDICULOUS.

FREE-FLOATING ANGER...A SERIES OF MASS MURDERERS, SOME OF WHOM WERE ALSO CULT LEADERS.

CHARLIE MANSON, YOU'RE A PIKER!

AND, MAYBE FROM DRUGS, OR FROM TV, OR FROM NUKE-THINK (SEE P.184) OR FROM AN INABILITY TO LOOK VIETNAM IN THE FACE— THE **PERCEPTION GAP.** THIS IS THE NOTION THAT PERCEPTION IS AS IMPORTANT AS REALITY, IF THERE IS A REALITY.

I CAN PACKAGE THAT!

166

AND THEN THERE WAS WOMEN'S LIBERATION

REMEMBER THAT CHANT, "GIRLS SAY YES TO BOYS WHO SAY NO"? THIS CHANT OFFENDED SOME GIRLS!

NO!

NO!

HEY, GIRLS! I SAID "NO!"

MALE CHAUVINISTS IN THE ANTI-WAR MOVEMENT HOGGED THE LEADERSHIP ROLES AND GENERALLY BELITTLED WOMEN.

ER— I THINK...

DOES ANYONE HEAR A VOICE? I DON'T HEAR A VOICE!

ALSO— THE SEXUAL REVOLUTION CREATED THE **MINISKIRT** (DESIGNED BY A WOMAN, NO LESS!). THIS WAS LIBERATION?

((FIDGET

TUG

SQUIRM

MOVEMENT WOMEN, EVEN SOME WITH GOOD LEGS, DENOUNCED THE MINI AS SLAVE CLOTHES!

ONLY PANTS ARE POLITICALLY CORRECT!

UNLESS EVERYONE WEARS LEOTARDS & TIGHTS!

LIKE THEIR ABOLITIONIST SISTERS OF 1848, MODERN FEMINISTS REACTED FIRST TO MALE CHAUVINISM IN THE BROADER MOVEMENT. SMALL CONSCIOUSNESS-RAISING (C.R.) GROUPS SPONTANEOUSLY FORMED ALL OVER THE COUNTRY.

CONSPIRE

VENT

EXPLORE

MEDITATE

WOMEN'S LIBERATIONISTS REJECTED SEXUAL OBJECTIFICATION, SEXUAL COMPETITION, BEAUTY PAGEANTS, STRUCTURAL UNDERGARMENTS, FEMALE PASSIVITY, INFANTILE BEHAVIOR, AND MINDLESS SUPPORTIVENESS. THE SLOGAN WAS:

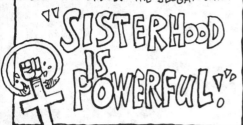

"SISTERHOOD IS POWERFUL!"

INDEED — SO IMPRESSED WERE THEY TO DISCOVER EACH OTHER'S WHOLE PERSONALITIES, THAT SOME FEMINISTS FELL IN LOVE — WITH EACH OTHER!!

THEIR SLOGAN: "A WOMAN WITHOUT A MAN IS LIKE A FISH WITHOUT A BICYCLE!"

THE C.R. GROUPS COALESCED INTO AN IMPRESSIVE ARRAY OF NATIONAL ORGANIZATIONS AND PUBLICATIONS.

MS. MAGAZINE FOUNDER GLORIA STEINEM

SOME OF THEIR GOALS:
- ANTI-DISCRIMINATION LAWS
- EQUAL RIGHTS AMENDMENT
- ABORTION ON DEMAND
- EQUAL PAY FOR EQUAL WORK
- PROSECUTION OF WIFE-BEATERS
- MORE SENSITIVE MEN

A RETURN TO GODDESS-WORSHIP!

B-BUT WE'RE MEN!

NOT TO BE OUTDONE IN SENSITIVITY, HOMOSEXUAL MEN CAME OUT PROUDLY, AND **GAY LIBERATION** WAS BORN.

IT'S GOOD TO BE DIFFERENT

IT'S GOOD TO BE DIFFE...

IT'S GO...

SEE? CASTRO STREET! PROOF OF A COMMIE PLOT!

IT'S ALL THIS PRESSURE TO BE SENSITIVE THAT ACCOUNTS FOR THE AWKWARD HUGGING THAT GOES ON NOW...

CAN I LET GO YET?

169

THE ECOLOGY MOVEMENT

'60'S SPACECRAFT BEAMED HOME THE FIRST PHOTOS OF THE WHOLE EARTH. UNTIL THEN, NO ONE HAD REALIZED HOW BEAUTIFUL, BLUE, SMALL, AND FRAGILE IT LOOKED...

SCIENTISTS SUDDENLY WOKE UP TO GLOBAL PROBLEMS: ACID RAIN; SMOG; PAVING OVER FOREST, MARSH, AND FARM; WATER AND SOIL POLLUTION; DESERTIFI-CATION; RADIOACTIVE WASTE; CONSUMPTION OF NON-RENEWABLE RESOURCES LIKE METALS AND FUELS; DESTRUCTION OF OZONE BY AEROSOL CANS; THE GREENHOUSE EFFECT... ADD YOUR OWN!

IT WAS DISCOVERED
THAT DOLPHINS
WERE AS INTELLIGENT
AS HUMAN BEINGS—
THAT WHALES
SANG SONGS!!

BUT WE
PUT OUR MINDS
TO SOMETHING
IMPORTANT—
HAVING FUN!

THE CONCEPT OF HUMANITY'S
DOMINION OVER NATURE
GAVE WAY TO ONE OF
INTERDEPENDENCE AND
HARMONY — THE IDEA OF AN

ECOSYSTEM.

THE DETAILS INCLUDED:
- RECYCLING
- ORGANIC FARMING
- POLLUTION CONTROL
- ALTERNATIVE ENERGY SOURCES
- CONSERVATION
- "SMALL IS BEAUTIFUL"
- WILDLIFE PROTECTION

⇨ ON A GLOBAL SCALE!!

HUMANS,
BLESS 'EM—
THEY TRY SO
HARD!!

WHAT REALLY BROUGHT THIS HOME TO AMERICANS WAS THE **OIL CRISIS.**

OIL-PRODUCING NATIONS, MINDFUL THAT THEIR RESERVES WOULD RUN OUT SOMEDAY, FORMED A CARTEL TO RAISE PRICES. THIS WAS THE **O**RGANIZATION OF **P**ETROLEUM **E**XPORTING **C**OUNTRIES.

THE RESULT IN THE U.S.A.:

DOLLAR REGULAR.

IT'S THE BEGINNING OF THE END...

GAS AND FUEL BILLS SUDDENLY DOUBLED AND TRIPLED. THE PRICE OF EVERYTHING THAT DEPENDED ON OIL FOR PRODUCTION OR TRANSPORTATION— I.E., EVERYTHING — WENT UP AND UP AND UP AND

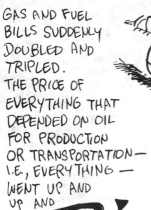

UP!

RECESSION AND INFLATION TOGETHER! A FIRST!

KA K

THE ECONOMY STAGNATED...

BURP

AMERICANS TURNED TO FUEL-EFFICIENT JAPANESE CARS, LEAVING DETROIT TO CHOKE ON THEIR EXHAUST.

SOME POLITICIANS ANNOUNCED THAT WE HAD ENTERED AN

ERA OF LIMITS.

LIMITS ON RESOURCES, GROWTH, AND WEALTH.

CALIF. GOV. JERRY "MOONBEAM" BROWN

LIMITS ALSO EXISTED ON U.S. POWER ABROAD: VIETNAM PROVED THAT! AFTER VIETNAM, REVOLUTIONS FOLLOWED IN LAOS, CAMBODIA, ETHIOPIA, ANGOLA, GUINEA-BISSAU, MOZAMBIQUE, SOUTH YEMEN, IRAN, NICARAGUA...

ANOTHER GLOBAL EVENT!

ANTI-AMERICANISM RAN HIGH, BECAUSE WHEREVER YOU LOOKED, THE U.S. OPPOSED POPULAR GOVERNMENTS AND BACKED DICTATORS:

GIT THEM COMMES!

THE PHILIPPINES?
THE DICTATOR MARCOS

S. KOREA?
THE DICTATOR CHUN

NICARAGUA?
THE " SOMOZA

GREECE?
THE COLONELS

IRAN?
A SHAH, FOR HEAVEN'S SAKE!

ARABIA?
A KING...

BETWEEN DEMOCRATIC INDIA AND AUTOCRATIC PAKISTAN? WE LIKE PAKISTAN... DEMOCRATIC CHILE? NIXON'S CIA TOPPLED PRESIDENT ALLENDE AND INSTALLED THE MONSTROUS PINOCHET.

BUT WE LIKE THE DEMOCRACIES OF ISRAEL AND SOUTH AFRICA!

AFTER THE VIETNAM HORROR, THE U.S. BACKED OFF THE HEAVY-HANDED IMPERIAL ACTION. NIXON'S SUCCESSOR, GERALD FORD, WAS THE ONLY PRESIDENT SINCE WORLD WAR II NOT TO CONSIDER ALERTING THE NUCLEAR FORCES.

I COULDN'T FIND THE BUTTON.

IT'S O.K. AH'M NOT A YANKEE... AH'M FROM GEORGIA...

HAVE SOME PEANUTS.

THE NEXT PRESIDENT, JIMMY CARTER, SENT AID TO THE NEW NICARAGUAN GOVERNMENT, WHOSE ANTHEM CALLS YANKEES THE "ENEMIES OF MANKIND."*

BUT EVEN CARTER COULDN'T DEAL WITH THE FUNDAMENTALIST ISLAMIC REVOLUTIONARIES IN IRAN. THEY COMPARED THE U.S. WITH SATAN (UNFAVORABLY).

JUST TRY AND BE FRIENDS WITH US!

THE IRANIANS SEIZED THE U.S. EMBASSY IN TEHRAN, HOLDING 50 PEOPLE HOSTAGE...

*BUT ONLY IN THE SECOND VERSE, SO PROBABLY NOBODY KNOWS IT...

DESPITE INTENSIVE NEGOTIATIONS, CARTER FAILED TO FREE THE HOSTAGES IN TIME FOR THE 1980 ELECTION. A NEWSPAPER EDITORIAL DESCRIBED HIS SPEECHES AS "MUSH FROM THE WIMP."

WRING
WRING
WRING

AND SO THE ELECTORATE BROUGHT IN A NEW MAN WHO WAS ALSO OLD —

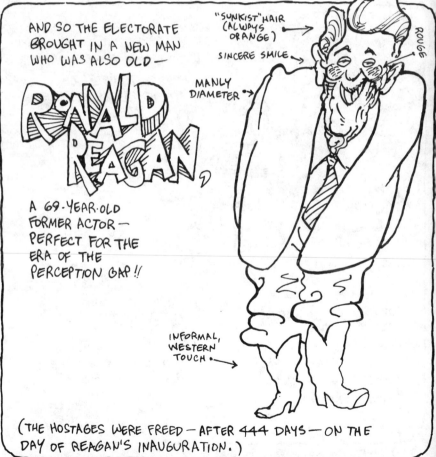

RONALD REAGAN

A 69·YEAR·OLD FORMER ACTOR — PERFECT FOR THE ERA OF THE PERCEPTION GAP!!

"SUNKIST" HAIR (ALWAYS ORANGE)

ROUGE

SINCERE SMILE

MANLY DIAMETER

INFORMAL, WESTERN TOUCH.

(THE HOSTAGES WERE FREED — AFTER 444 DAYS — ON THE DAY OF REAGAN'S INAUGURATION.)

REAGAN'S SUPPORTERS CALLED HIM FIRM AND CONSISTENT. HIS DETRACTORS SAID HIS IDEAS HAD BEEN FIXED IN STONE LONG AGO.

REAGAN BELIEVED IN LIMITS, TOO, THE OLD-FASHIONED KIND: ON TAXES, FEDERAL SPENDING, AND GOVERNMENT REGULATIONS. THE REAGAN ADMINISTRATION BEGAN TO CUT — POLLUTION CONTROLS, FOOD STAMP BENEFITS, MEDICARE AND EDUCATION OUTLAYS, AND TAXES.

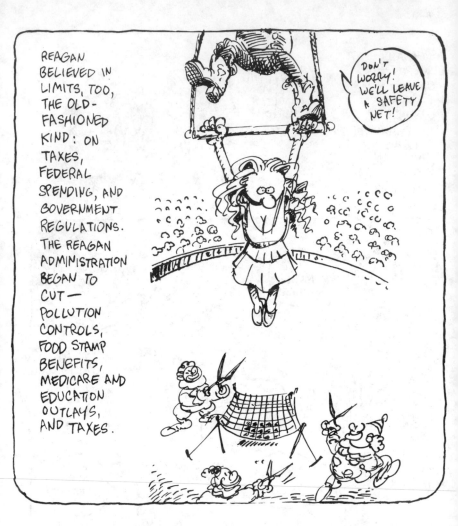

DON'T WORRY! WE'LL LEAVE A SAFETY NET!

MEANWHILE, HE CALLED FOR MORE SHIPS, MORE TANKS, MORE PLANES, MORE NUKES!

MORE $500 HAMMERS!

AND THE RESULT?

TAX CUTS AND MILITARY CONTRACTS STIMULATED BUSINESS... DEREGULATION BROUGHT SOME PRICES DOWN... OPEC, WEAKENED BY THE IRANIAN REVOLUTION AND WORLDWIDE CONSERVATION, COULDN'T HOLD OIL PRICES UP... SO THE ECONOMY PICKED UP— MIRACULOUSLY WITHOUT INFLATION !!

EEHA!

BUT,

AS IN THE 1920's, THE RICH GOT RICHER AND THE POOR GREW MORE NUMEROUS... A GET-RICH-QUICK MENTALITY PREVAILED... "JUNK" BONDS OF QUESTIONABLE VALUE CIRCULATED... BANKS TREMBLED... STEEL AND AUTO PLANTS CLOSED WHILE BURGER CHAINS EXPANDED... FARMERS LOST THEIR LAND... FEDERAL BUDGET DEFICITS HIT ALL-TIME HIGHS... POVERTY, HUNGER, AND HOMELESSNESS SPREAD. WHERE WAS THE "SAFETY NET"?

WELL, WE ONLY CUT AWAY PART OF IT...

179

THE '80'S:

≈WUP≈ IT'S ANOTHER HOMELESS PERSON... ICKY... DISGUSTINGLY DIRTY... DON'T STARE... IT'S NOT POLITE... BUT BETTER KEEP AN EYE ON HER, IN CASE SHE MAKES ANY SUDDEN MOVES... O.K....BUT... WHAT *IS* THAT STRANGE SENSATION IN MY CHEST?? AM I HAVING A HEART ATTACK?? AAAGH — WORSE... IT'S...IT'S... SYMPATHY... @#★$!! WHY DO I HAVE TO BE *PUT* IN THIS POSITION? DAMMIT! WHAT CAN *I* DO, ANYWAY?... I KNOW... I'LL SPEAK TO HER...

GREAT GOD, WOMAN! TAKE RESPONSIBILITY FOR YOURSELF!

MUMBLE MUTTER MUTTER MUMBLE

180

BUT NEVER MIND! THE MIGHTY MILITARY MACHINE WAS BACK IN MOTION!! IN 1984, REAGAN ORDERED THE MARINES INTO LEBANON, WITH NO CLEAR MISSION EXCEPT TO BE A PRESENCE.

TWO HUNDRED OF THEM WERE BLOWN UP IN THEIR BEDS... BUT NEVER MIND! REAGAN ORDERED THE NAVY TO OVERTHROW THE MARXIST GOVERNMENT OF GRENADA.

THE ELECTORATE EVIDENTLY PREFERRED REAGAN'S DEAD MARINES TO CARTER'S LIVE HOSTAGES... HE WAS OVERWHELMINGLY RE-ELECTED IN NOVEMBER...

THE POST-VIETNAM SYNDROME STILL RESTRAINED REAGAN FROM INVADING NICARAGUA, SO HE SECRETLY RAISED MONEY FROM FOREIGN GOVERNMENTS TO FUND THE COUNTER-REVOLUTIONARIES.

SEE NO EVIL, HEAR NO EVIL, RECALL NO EVIL...

AID THE CONTRA

THIS THIRD-WORLD TURMOIL, SAID REAGAN, STEMMED FROM THE **SOVIET MENACE.** THE SOVIET MENACE WAS EITHER AN OCTOPUS, A CANCER, OR SOME FALLING DOMINOES.

IT'S A CANCEROUS DOMINO WITH EIGHT LEGS!

AS EVERYONE WHO HADN'T LEARNED ANYTHING SINCE THE '50's KNEW, THE OCTOPUS LIVED IN MOSCOW...

AND WHEN IT CAME TO MOSCOW, THERE WAS ONLY ONE WEAPON' WORTH TALKING ABOUT—

NUKES, GOD BLESS 'EM!

IN THE BEGINNING WAS THE BOMB... IT WAS DROPPED FROM A BOMBER... THEN CAME SPUTNIK, WHICH SHOWED THAT A MISSILE COULD GO ANYWHERE IN HALF AN HOUR... BOMBS BECAME "WARHEADS"... THEN CAME SHORT-, MEDIUM-, AND LONG-RANGE MISSILES... MISSILES WITH MANY INDEPENDENTLY TARGETED WARHEADS ("MIRV'S")... AIR-, GROUND-, AND SEA-LAUNCHED MISSILES... CRUISE MISSILES... NEUTRON BOMBS, BEAM WEAPONS, X-RAY LASERS, ELECTROMAGNETIC PULSE DEVICES... 60,000 WARHEADS IN ALL — ENOUGH TO DESTROY THE WORLD 50 TIMES OVER!

SURELY YOU DON'T THINK THEY ALL WORK?

THE DANGER IS SO OBVIOUS THAT THE SUPERPOWERS HAVE REACHED SEVERAL AGREEMENTS TO MANAGE THE MENACE... THE TEST-BAN TREATY ('63), THE ANTI-BALLISTIC MISSILE TREATY ('72), STRATEGIC ARMS LIMITATION TREATIES I & II ('72 AND '79)... UNDER THE CIRCUMSTANCES, CLOSE COOPERATION WITH THE ADVERSARY IS ESSENTIAL!

GOOD — NOW, LEONID, WOULD YOU PUT ON THE OCTOPUS MASK FOR THE PHOTOGRAPHERS?

183

AND SO WE LIVE WITH THE PARADOXES OF THE NUCLEAR AGE.

FOR EXAMPLE: YOU CAN'T ACTUALLY **USE** NUKES, WITHOUT RISKING PLANETARY DESTRUCTION... YOU CAN ONLY **THREATEN** TO USE THEM!

ANOTHER PARADOX: ANTI-MISSILE DEFENSES CAN DECREASE SECURITY. WHY? BECAUSE DEFENSES SEND A SIGNAL TO YOUR ENEMY THAT YOU THINK THAT NUCLEAR WAR IS SURVIVABLE... SO YOU'RE MORE WILLING TO RISK A FIRST STRIKE... SO YOUR ENEMY IS TEMPTED TO STRIKE FIRST — IN SELF-DEFENSE!!

AND THEN CAME REAGAN, WHO ANNOUNCED THAT NUCLEAR WAR WAS "WINNABLE."

HE ABANDONED THE ANTI-BALLISTIC MISSILE LOGIC AND PROPOSED "STAR WARS," DESCRIBED AS A DEFENSIVE SATELLITE SENSOR AND WEAPON SYSTEM, DESIGNED TO DESTROY INCOMING MISSILES AND CONTROLLED BY THE WORLD'S MOST COMPLEX COMPUTER SOFTWARE — WHICH HAS TO WORK PERFECTLY THE FIRST TIME!

THOUSANDS OF SCIENTISTS REFUSED TO WORK ON IT... THEY SAY IT CAN'T WORK... BUT STILL THE RUSSIANS ARE SCARED — AND WHY? BECAUSE STAR WARS HAS **OFFENSIVE** POTENTIAL! WE'RE TALKING DEATH BEAMS FROM SPACE HERE!!

WELL! THE WORLD HAS CERTAINLY CHANGED SINCE 1776!

WE FACE CHALLENGES UNDREAMED OF THEN: TECHNOLOGICAL THREATS TO LIFE, LIMB, AND PRIVACY; ENVIRONMENTAL PRESERVATION; BUREAUCRACY IN GOVERNMENT AND BUSINESS; SOCIALISM, UNIONS, AND OTHER ASSERTIONS OF WORKERS' RIGHTS; AND THE RIGHTS OF WOMEN.

AND, AT THE SAME TIME, THE FOUNDING FATHERS' ISSUES REMAIN LIVE ONES: RACIAL JUSTICE, RESTRAINTS ON GOVERNMENT POWER, FREE EXPRESSION OF IDEAS, RELIGIOUS TOLERATION, SECURITY OF OUR HOMES AND SELVES, ECONOMIC JUSTICE...

AND MIRACULOUSLY, THE FOUNDERS' CONSTITUTION ALSO REMAINS, TO GUARANTEE EVERY CITIZEN SOME VOICE AND INFLUENCE IN FACING THESE PROBLEMS.

NOW THAT'S EXCITING!

HOW WILL IT ALL TURN OUT, ONE WONDERS...?

186

IN ONE SENSE, THE HISTORIAN IS THE LUCKIEST OF AUTHORS: UNLIKE THE NOVELIST, WHO ENDS A BOOK AT THE END, THE HISTORIAN ALWAYS FINISHES IN THE MIDDLE OF THE STORY. NO TIDY, PAT CONCLUSIONS HERE!
IN FACT, I THINK I'LL END THE BOOK IN THE MIDDLE OF A...
END

BIBLIOGRAPHY

BAILEY, T.A., *THE AMERICAN PAGEANT*, 4TH ED., LEXINGTON, MA, 1971, HEATH; ENDS OPTIMISTICALLY JUST BEFORE WATERGATE.

BERNSTEIN, I., *THE LEAN YEARS*, N.Y., PLENUM, 1960; LABOR IN THE 1920's.

BOYER, R., + MORAIS, H., *LABOR'S UNTOLD STORY*, N.Y., UE, 1955; UNITED ELECTRICAL WORKERS, 1955; USEFUL BUT BIASED.

BRECHER, J., *STRIKE!*, SAN FRANCISCO, STRAIGHT ARROW BOOKS, 1972; FULL ACCOUNT OF 1877; MAKES A CASE THAT DIRECT ACTION, NOT UNIONS, HELPS WORKERS.

BRODIE, F., *THADDEUS STEVENS, SCOURGE OF THE SOUTH*, N.Y., NORTON, 1959; FINE BIO.

CODY, W.F. *AN AUTOBIOGRAPHY OF BUFFALO BILL*, N.Y., COSMOPOLITAN, 1920; A LIFE OR A LIE?

CONNELL, E., *SON OF THE MORNING STAR*, N.Y., HARPER & ROW, 1984; RAMBLING BUT THOROUGH ACCOUNT OF CUSTER, THE SIOUX, AND THEIR MEETING.

CRONON, E.D., *BLACK MOSES: THE STORY OF MARCUS GARVEY*. MADISON, WISC, U. OF WISC., 1969.

DE TOLEDANO, R., *J. EDGAR HOOVER*, NEW ROCHELLE, N.Y., ARLINGTON HOUSE, 1973; UNCRITICAL IF NOT WORSHIPFUL.

DOYLE, E., + WEISS, S., *THE VIETNAM EXPERIENCE*, IN SEVERAL VOLUMES, BOSTON, BOSTON PUBLISHING CO, 1984; LOADS OF PIX AND INFO.

DU BOIS, W.E.B., *BLACK RECONSTRUCTION IN AMERICA*, N.Y., ATHENEUM, 1979; SCHOLARLY YET IMPASSIONED.

FRIED, R.M., *MEN AGAINST McCARTHY*, N.Y., COLUMBIA U. PRESS, 1976; THE "MEN" IN QUESTION, MOSTLY DEMOCRATS, INCLUDE SEN. MARGARET CHASE SMITH.

GALBRAITH, J.K., *THE AFFLUENT SOCIETY*, 3RD ED., N.Y., NEW AMERICAN LIBRARY, 1978; A CLASSIC.

GALBRAITH, J.K., *THE AGE OF UNCERTAINTY*, BOSTON, HOUGHTON MIFFLIN, 1977; BASED ON A TV SERIES.

GIAP, V.N., *BANNER OF PEOPLE'S WAR: THE PARTY'S MILITARY LINE*, N.Y., PRAEGER, 1970; BY NORTH VIETNAM'S TOP GENERAL.

GIAP, V.N., *THE MILITARY ART OF PEOPLE'S WAR*, N.Y., MONTHLY REVIEW PRESS, 1970.

GOFF, S., + SAUNDERS, R., *BROTHERS: BLACK SOLDIERS IN THE NAM*, NOVATO, PRESIDIO PRESS, 1982; HIGHLY EVOCATIVE FIRST-HAND ACCOUNTS.

JABLONSKI, E., *A PICTORIAL HISTORY OF THE WORLD WAR II YEARS*, N.Y., DOUBLEDAY, 1977; BETTER ON EUROPE THAN THE PACIFIC.

KAKU, M., + AXELROD, D., *TO WIN A NUCLEAR WAR*, BOSTON, SOUTH END PRESS, 1987; REVEALS NIXON'S "OPERATION DUCK HOOK."

LEARY, T., *FLASHBACKS*, L.A., TARCHER, 1983; A MODERN MENTAL BUFFALO BILL.

LENS, S., *THE FUTILE CRUSADE*, CHICAGO, QUADRANGLE, 1964; ARGUES AGAINST MINDLESS ANTI-COMMUNISM.

LENS, S., *STRIKEMAKERS AND STRIKEBREAKERS*, N.Y., DUTTON, 1985; AN UNUSUAL CHILDREN'S BOOK.

PHILBRICK, H., *I LED THREE LIVES*, N.Y., McGRAW-HILL, 1952.

POWERS, R.G., *SECRECY AND POWER, THE LIFE OF J EDGAR HOOVER*, N.Y., FREE PRESS, 1987; BALANCES DE TOLEDANO.

PRATT, J.W., *A HISTORY OF U.S. FOREIGN POLICY*, N.Y., PRENTICE-HALL, 1955; FINE & JUDICIOUS, AS FAR AS IT GOES, BUT VERY QUIET ON THE U.S.S.R.

SALVATORE, N., *EUGENE V. DEBS, CITIZEN & SOCIALIST*, URBANA, U. OF ILLINOIS, 1982.

SCHULKE, F., + McPHEE, P., *KING REMEMBERED*, N.Y., POCKET BOOKS, 1986; GOOD PICTORIAL RECORD OF MARTIN LUTHER KING, JR.

STONE, I.F., *THE HIDDEN HISTORY OF THE KOREAN WAR*, N.Y., MONTHLY REVIEW PRESS, 1952; A MUST READ.

UNITED PRESS INTERNATIONAL, *FOUR DAYS: THE HISTORICAL RECORD OF THE DEATH OF PRESIDENT KENNEDY*, N.Y., AMERICAN HERITAGE, 1964.

ZINN, H., *A PEOPLE'S HISTORY OF THE UNITED STATES*, N.Y., HARPER & ROW, 1980.

INDEX

ABOUT THE AUTHOR:

LARRY GONICK, THE OVEREDUCATED CARTOONIST, STILL LIVES IN SAN FRANCISCO WITH HIS FAMILY, WHICH ONLY SEEMS TO GROW LARGER, BOTH INDIVIDUALLY AND COLLECTIVELY.

By the year 2000, 2 out of 3 Americans could be illiterate.

It's true.

Today, 75 million adults...about one American in three, can't read adequately. And by the year 2000, U.S. News & World Report envisions an America with a literacy rate of only 30%.

Before that America comes to be, you can stop it...by joining the fight against illiteracy today.

Call the Coalition for Literacy at toll-free **1-800-228-8813** and volunteer.

**Volunteer
Against Illiteracy.
The only degree you need
is a degree of caring.**

Ad Council Coalition for Literacy